REUNION

A Spiritual Travelogue

ABOUT THE COVER: This image graced the restroom door at the bus station in Varna, on the Black Sea, something like the plastic card in the pouch in front of your seat on an airplane explaining where the exits are and how to put on your oxygen mask when if falls from the ceiling. It seems to be designed for country folk who may never have used modern plumbing and only a Turkish john (two footpads and a hole in the floor you squat over to do your business.) Sit there and relax is the proper position. Read your newspaper or your Koran or your Bible or what have you. Do not stand on the toilet bowl, do not wash your hair in the toilet bowel. The last injunction isn't quite clear. No yogi's permitted? Anyhow, bottom line, when you gotta go, you gotta go. People live differently in different cultures.

Publications

COMES LOVE, Poets Choice Publishing, 2015

WMD, A Memoir, Poets Choice Publishing, 2013

CROSSING OVER, Editor of the bilingual edition of William Meredith's poetry with serigraph illustrations by Sooky Maniquantm, 2012, Little Red Tree Publishing.

I HEAR ALWAYS THE DOGS ON THE HOSPITAL ROOF, 2012. Edited and introduced the first William Meredith Award for Poetry given to David Fisher. Little Red Tree Publishing.

THE REVENANT, 2010 poems. Little Red Tree Publishing, New London, Ct. July 2010

LEGACY, 2007 Poems in a private edition of 222 copies

ECHOES, November 2007 Poems for William, 2004, Vivisphere Publishing, Poughkeepsie, N.Y.

2004 MARATHON, 2001 (Reprinting of previous W.W. Norton edition, 1989) Vivisphere Publishing, Poughkeepsie, N.Y. (Www.Vivisphere.com telephone 800-724-1100)

ECHOES, 1989 an art folio, book contains six poems by William Meredith and six poems by Richard Harteis with twelve especially designed Illustrations by Stoimen Stoilov in an edition of thirty copies, each signed and numbered by the artists.

2000 PROVENCE, New and Selected Poems, 2000, Vivisphere Publishing, Pougkeepsie, N.Y. (www.Vivisphere.com Telephone 800-724-1100)

SAPPHIRE DAWN, 2000, Vivisphere Publishing, Poughkeepsie, N.Y. (www.vivisphere.com) 2000

TIME BOMB, 1999, Bulgarski Pisatel (ISBN: 954-443-3333, distributed in the United States by Carnegie Mellon University Press) Poems by Krassin Himmirsky, translations in English by Richard Harteis

1999 LARGO, 1999, AngoBoy Publishing, Sofia, Bulgaria (ISBN:954-9885-690) Poems by Petar Parvanov, Edited with an introduction by Richard Harteis

1999 THE WHITE ISLAND, 1998 Orpheus House, Paris, Sofia

1998 KEEPING HEART, (English/Bulgarian Bi-lingual edition) 1996, Orpheus House, Sofia and Paris, fourth Edition, 1998, Poetry

KEEPING HEART, 1994, Orpheus House, Sofia and Paris 1994

WINDOW ON THE BLACK SEA, 1992, Carnegie-Mellon University Press. Anthology of Bulgaria poetry in translation. Edited in collaboration with William Meredith, 1992

MARATHON, W.W. Norton Inc., 1989

INTERNAL GEOGRAPHY, 1989 Carnegie-Mellon University Press, 1987

MOROCCO JOURNAL, 1981, Love, Work, Play, Carnegie-Mellon University Press

FOURTEEN WOMEN, Three Rivers Press, 1979. Second edition, 1980.

REUNION

A Spiritual Travelogue

RICHARD HARTEIS

Poets' Choice Publishing

Copyright © 2017 Poets' Choice Publishing
All rights reserved
Printed in the United States of America

Consultant work: www.WilliamMeredithFoundation.org

Bulk discounts available through www.Poets-Choice.com
Library of Congress Cataloging-in-Publication Data pending
ISBN: 978-0-9972629-3-3

Poets' Choice Publishing
337 Kitemaug Road
Uncasville, CT 06382
Poets-Choice.com

REUNION

A Spiritual Travelogue

For Bob and Ellen

TABLE OF CONTENTS

Preface	9
1. Rumination	15
2. Harteis Family Reunion	19
3. Cataract Surgery	23
4. Daphne	25
5. Email Chain	29
6. Crossing the Rubicon	33
7. Russians	36
8. Septic Garden	38
9. Labor Day	47
10. Letter to Mikey	50
11. Met at Geneva	52
12. Provincetown	61
13. Sting is in Tuscany	71
14. Day Trip	79
15. Sunday Bloody Sunday	96
16. Sofia, Here I Come	105
17. Lunch with the Lion	114
18. Sozopol	126
19. Varna	146
20. Return to Sofia	162
21. Meet the Press	169
22. Epilog – Supermoon	176

Reunion.

RICHARD HARTEIS

PREFACE
It is always so moving when the guy stamps your passport
and says, "Welcome Home."

Like a recent hotel commercial featuring nervous, would-be bridesmaids and young businessmen contemplating a trade show, "Should I stay or should I go," was a snappy little tune that played out all summer long on TV. I had been bombarded by emails from old classmates asking if I were going to return to Fribourg, Switzerland for the 50th reunion of our Junior Year Abroad from Georgetown. At the Courtyard opening last night, Dave pointed out that the surprising thing about reunions was how much older the OTHER people looked. Nancy Frankel said that when she went to her 60th reunion, people had to have name tags with photos of what they looked like all those years ago so you could identify them. But as Gertrude Stein has pointed out, "We are always the same age inside."

I wasn't even sure I would still recognize these old classmates, and wondered if we would be provided with name tag and photo of how we looked when we were young and beautiful, learning how to make love, preening among ourselves, determining what our position was in the pack and who might be the alpha male, figuring out our relationship to money and planning for our future, learning how to deal with tragedy for the first time on a personal level, that we were not immortal, that the thread tying us to life was very fragile and could be severed in an instant.

John Carr, Ed Papantonio, Charles Timberlake, Bob Nish, Bill Wisniewski, Mike Fitzgerald, Richard Harteis, William J Grohs.

Mary Jo (Day) Knauf, Michèle Longino, Lynn Troy, Kathy (Wessels) Cook, Maureen (O'Brien) Hurley, Jan (Barnes) Hanson at far right

The SPOUSES, LEFT TO RIGHT: Jennifer Strand (Wisniewski), Gwen Grohs, Marilyn Fitzgerald, Anne Papantonio, Nona Carr, Rob Cook, Pat Timberlake, Klaus Hanson

For some, it was "golden days in the sunshine of our flowered youth." For others, like myself, who adopted something like the current Goth style of teenagers living skeptically on the periphery of the "in" crowd, it was not the formative year confirming rank and status that would carry one on to a successful career in banking, jurisprudence, art administration. I am still not a household word, nor imagine will I ever be. My name, like Keats may be "writ in water," as it says on his tombstone. And as I age, it matters less and less.

Now we came together to see what had become of each other since those privileged days of raclette and fondue dinners in the upper chambers of the Café au Midi, or afternoon tea and cookies in our chambers at the Foyer St. Justin, the dormitory where the boys lived and the Villa des Fougères, chez les girls. In the end, with a little help from Bob and Ellen Storck who could not go, I went.

Villa des Fougères   **Foyer St. Justin**

But it was not just a long weekend in Switzerland that I was contemplating. Earlier in the summer I made the same decision about a family reunion in Pennsylvania to check out the western branch of the tribe gathering at cousin at Jerry's Horse Farm. And this nostalgia for the past deepened as I approached my 70th birthday and ruminated on what life had in store for me in the remaining years, what I had accomplished to date." Ten more good ones," was the constant refrain from my dad, though he didn't meet that goal as his heart leapt, and he fell from the breakfast table.

Harteis family Reunion at Jerry's Horse Farm

As I had managed to get my butt to Europe, I decided to continue on to my second homeland, Bulgaria, to carry some of my partner's ashes to the Rila Monastery. For two years William and I had braved the winters and economic depression of Blagoevgrad as professors at the American University in Blagoevgrad—I, the Fulbright poet in residence, he, as the guest former US Poet Laureate.

(ABOVE: Richard Harteis, President Julia Watkins, and William Meredith standing on the balcony of the President's Office at the American University in Bulgaria on the day of the presentation of William's honorary Ph.D.)

I wanted to have his spirit ride the wind in those mountains where we sometimes prayed and took refuge in the surrounding natural beauty. REUNION became a process for me as I met up with friends who had suddenly gone grey and were a little creaky, but had morphed into compassionate fellow pilgrims. Egged on by Grace Cavalieri: "Please bring us the past, otherwise we have nothing but the present," I decided to try to put things in perspective as a birthday gift to myself, but tried to remember Meister Echkart Tolle's injunction to live in the present: "There is no greater obstacle to God than time."

ECKHART TOLLE is a contemporary spiritual teacher who is not aligned with any particular religion or tradition. He writes with the timeless and uncomplicated clarity of the ancient spiritual masters and imparts a simple yet profound message: There is a way out of suffering and into peace. He is the author of Stillness Speaks and Practicing the Power of Now. He travels widely and lives in Vancouver, British Columbia.

Like a grade school boy whose first assignment in September was to write an account of "what I did last summer," REUNION became the senior version, a "spiritual" travelogue, part slide show of old haunts, part nostalgic beating of an aging heart taking it all in. I was putting away acorns in the attic of my soul against future winter snows and the natural entropy of a world at rest. Short and sweet, shorter and shorter the summers. Where did they go, the endless summer's when one got bored and almost didn't mind that school was starting up again? Shorter yes, but with luck sweeter too, with less and less precious runway as we all prepare for landing.

1. RUMINATION

I sent Gracie the first page of this reunion journal yesterday, and here is how my soul sister replied:

OH YOU ARE IMMORTAL. PLEASE PLEASE BRING US THE PAST. PLEASE. OTHERWISE WE HAVE NOTHING BUT THE PRESENT

To which I pointed out, "The present ain't so bad. Do you really think People will be interested in this reunion and my take on the past? I'm like you Gracie, I just keep writing 'em. I saw a message on Facebook recently which read, 'life should be more than just paying bills and then you die.' August 18th, I will be 70 and I'm going to keep that message in mind. I love you, Richard"

The exchange sent me to Eckhart Tolle once again who stresses the crucial importance of NOW. "The whole essence of Zen consists in walking along the razor's edge of Now – to be so utterly, so completely in the present that no problem, no suffering, nothing that is not *who you are* in your essence, can survive in you. In the Now, in the absence of time, all your problems dissolve. Suffering needs time; it can not survive in the Now." And Tolle quotes other teachers to re-inforce his point:

"Past and future veil God from our sight; burn up both of them with fire."
Rumi

"Time is what keeps the light from reaching us. There is no greater obstacle to God than time."
Meister Echkart

I hear these words as though someone were calling from the other side of a lake on a dark night with a full moon, and me without canoe or strength enough to reach the other side. I have been standing on that shore for decades now, and the voice continues to trouble my heart.....

(PA – though I imagine my cousin's horse farm will have a Texas feeling to it) and bring some sort of home-made dessert. So, a double reunion is in store for me, and it seems I'll be living in the past all summer long.

Lovely the way long-term memory leads the pack when you get older and leaves short term memory in the dust. This morning, out of the blue I recall the name of the journalist Ivalin Grevealov who took me to the soothsayer Vanga down near the Greek border and as the vapors rose over the volcano floor where she lived, my mind said to her: "Will I be wed to these mountains? Will I be born again?"

In this morning's acceptance note to cousin Jerry and his wife, I tried to lay the groundwork for my behavior: "I remember my mother telling us three subjects of conversation were not permitted: politics, religion and sex. These are the only things worth talking about, of course. But, I'll do my best to listen to my mother." - There are bound to moments when the election comes up, or the church's teaching on homosexuality – which could actually cover two of the forbidden topics. "Should I go or should I stay…" I sent Jerry a photo of Sydney dressed in her "support dog" outfit to prepare him for the fact that she'd be traveling with me, and another of the flowering wall of my terrace to camouflage the fact that I was preparing him for the fact that she'd be traveling with me.

Well, if you can't put up with a dog on a horse farm what kind of horse farm can it be? Seems that the western branch of the family has, "more money than God," a cliché my siblings are fond of repeating when they give me news of the Ebensburg Harteis'. Will this be a working farm, or a status symbol like a trophy wife for the Donald. "Should I stay or should I go?"

I remember sleeping with Jerry as a boy – on the farm all the boys were housed in the boys dorm (Aunt Ruth bore 14 living children) and the younger ones shared a bed with visiting cousins like me. Turns out I wasn't exactly pre-pubescent, and didn't sleep until it was time to milk the cows, wondering if he would touch the erection that had flowered in my tighty whities. Boy stuff, but a phase Freud says out of which I should normally have grown by then. Well, Freud's been somewhat debunked by Adler and others I believe. Look at America – same sex marriage legal in all 50 states, join the boy scouts if your gay and game. That many people who never moved on to loving their mother and wishing to murder their father? I think we are all part of the rainbow coalition at some level, somewhere along the spectrum. Alan Ginsberg used to carry a little ukulele around on occasion and sing, "Oh, everybody's just a little homosexual, who hasn't admired a boy in a baseball cap with rosy cheeks…." Or something like that.

We rode ponies bareback and when the horse would lower its head galloping down a hill, there was no way you could hold onto its mane. You were young enough and your bones were green enough not to break when your rolled over his head and into the alfalfa field. Very young, age five perhaps, I approached the ladies drinking tea on the poach holding a live weasel by the tail as it tried to reach up and bite the hand and wrist that held it. The ladies screamed at me, I let it drop, it ran beneath the house.

The family had grown so used to the smell of cow dung, they might have been living in a pine forest. Boots and Mackintoshes, lined up for travel to the barn, the odor permeating the mud room and the entire farm house. By end of summer, I didn't notice it any more than a cat lover notices the smell of the litter box in the bathroom.

The structuring of these ruminations has not been helped by the fact that the tenant knocked on my door at 9:00 after I had watered the garden and was just sitting down to write a nice, structured entry in this journal, and offered me a hit of the pot he was taking to get his day going. "Good stuff," he assured me.

Indeed. But it is time to cease and desist and prepare for my meeting with the Mayor tomorrow morning. That meeting perhaps for the last time.

2. HARTEIS RUNION

Dear Jerry, My neighbor Rita said to me once when I was debating how much of my life to include in a book I was writing, "Richad (New Enlgand, keep in mind), Richad, write what you want to write." And as I approach 70, so it is. Perhaps, it is unwise to send you this journal entry – I am writing an account of a reunion of my college classmates who were in Switzerland for our junior year abroad which will take place in September. And this reunion is another in what seems to be a summer of reunions as I approach 70. I hope you won't take offense in any part of it. And please know it comes with gratitude for the lovely event you hosted last weekend. We give an annual prize for poetry in William's name and I'd like to send it to you. It is really a beautiful poet. Is the Carpenter Road address is a good mailing address? Thanks again Jerry to you and Polly both for a great time. Richard

July 30, 2016

Through the pouring rain Saturday, a five-hoiur drive and really torrential rains driving through the hills of Pennsylvania. But, the rains came and went when I finally got to the pavilion on Jerry's farm beside the lake he created. A real lake, a big lake. And the sign read like The Ponderosa as drove up.

I met about a hundred people who all looked the same, same Harteis eyes and little lisp as they spoke – except for one beauty who looked Persian who accepted a puff from my vapor pen. "Sativa," he said knowingly. I floated around, there but not really there, taking it all in. "Here's cousin Richie, he's the intellectual in the family. You should google him sometime." Who wouldn't love it.

All my snobbery about being an East coast Harteis as opposed to the tacky, Amway fortunes my western Pa cousins seem to have made pyramiding up to diamond status or whatever dissipated like mist after the rain. Just jealousy on our part?

"Are you a charlatan," I asked Jerry after a certain amount of gin and pot. "Are you like Donald Trump?" And he, training, natural disposition, smiled the question away. I was hooked. Bug-eyed, like me and, a gentle person. Very glad to see this part of him and his beautiful wife Polly. Turns out these are pretty classy folk, and it was well worth the while to disabuse myself of the sort of prejudice I have been fed over the years.

I left copies of my book for some of the special cousins like Nancy. And I put them on the table for the silent auction. Wonder if they will be read, if I will ever publish this account. I heard very little political discussion – Just Tom who repeated the clichés about Hillary. But no one picked up the ball. I would have walked away, but no need. No one there was about to change his opinion of his candidate by anything I might say.

Some of the old grievances did float to the top—fights that took place decades before we moved east. I remember mother saying how Bernie looked after her when dad went to the war, her animus toward Larney who was the progenitor of this whole bunch. There were perhaps 5 women with the name of Ruth after his wife who bore 14 live children. Everyone agreeing she was a Saint. She came to my own father's funeral and all the arguments between those brothers and sisters were kept silent, the passion still moving them like the strong current stirring below the calm surface of a river. But she came. Fierce loyalty to her brother, her eyes silent but burning. And my mother's gratitude that she came. Woman to woman. Outliving their men, that final triumph.

So, there were horse rides, and a spread of food unlike any I have ever seen: barbequed ribs, chicken, 10 kinds of salads, peaches, pies, gobs, any kind of Harteis specialty you could think of. I watched as little groups of 10 or 15 took pictures of their particular family and I got a bit morose that my family was not there, that the two big loves of my life, my mother and William were both gone. Bob still smarting from the loss of his wife, Judy in San Diego monitoring one son's seizures, Barb with her own digestive troubles.

I drove away and didn't stay for the group photo. Back to the Red Roof Inn and my dog sharing the king-sized bed, getting it all dirty from her day romping with five other visiting dogs. She was better at it than I. Such a social, sweet character. A couple of bite marks in her ear, but not the worse for wear. She tore along the bank of the lake all day, muddy, joyful. Glad to be alive in some place she had never been before. At one point, one of the farm hands, a woman who was helping the children get into the saddle for horse rides, said "look at that dog, what a beautiful dog that is. What kind of dog is that. Look at her markings." Didn't compare to the beautiful babies that were being shown off throughout the day, God knows what my relationship to them might be, 5th something or other removed? But I tucked her comment away and went for a piece of blueberry pie, glad to have made the trip.

me and cousin Jerry

3. CATARACT SURGERY

August 5, 2016

This morning I am able to have coffee early, water, whatever I need. So, a big bowl of granola and playing with Sydney a little bit to celebrate. I'm looking out through a plastic eye patch like a jerry-rigged character from Road Warrior after yesterday's cataract surgery. One old lady in the waiting room calls it her Cadillac surgery and it sure does seem like it turned out to be a classy event. I'm getting myself put together bit by bit for the summer travel or the fall travel rather to Switzerland and Bulgaria. Do I want to make this small short visit to Bulgaria? Lyubomir looks very fragile now, that sort of startled, scared look that seems to be a tell-tale sign of Parkinson's, the same sort of look Fred Fisher had when I visited this summer.

How quickly we age, how inevitable. I recall standing on the Intracoastal walkway staring over at Donald Trump's Mar-A-Lago a little bit like Jay Gatsby staring at the green light on the other side of the water pining for Daisy and his dream of success in America, the same dream being played out now in Trump's Run for the presidency. Seems he is trying to undercut the results of the election even before it's happened, saying it's rigged. Half of America will believe him because they feel their lives are rigged too.

How did we get to be a nation of whiners and self-indulgent selfish spirits? Whatever happened the greatest generation? I think of the pilot in Williams poem who brings his shattered plane into the hangar, and reads the books that tell about weather over coffee and cake by himself and then flies off into the night and is never seen again.

Trump intuits this worst self we seem to have become, this sense of aggrievment, this national petulance. If he doesn't win things won't change in the culture, there will still be this underlying sense of wrong. Am I any better relishing his downfall? Such a vulgar thug. I remember jogging the Palm Beach streets bareback one day and dipped down Worth Avenue. A very old, purple-haired woman put her cane out in front of me, it was actually bejeweled as I recall, and scolded me in a heavy German accent, "you could be arrested for looking like that." That sense of entitlement the one tenth of one percent feel, as though they have an absolute right to cut you off in traffic because they have a Rolls-Royce. And this Trump claims to be the great champion of the middle class. Such hypocrisy. All his birther diatribe against Obama and his trophy wife who claims to have had an HB1. I remember getting such a visa for Natalia Himmirska or trying at least to get this Visa as she demanded. I recall you had to prove that no one else could do the job, that you had hired or advertised for someone to fill the job. There must certainly have been many sexy women willing to pose nude on the cover of a tabloid. It will be interesting to see what happens there.

Well, fall travel for the reunion continues to trouble my mind. I delve into the several tragedies that occurred during that junior year abroad. Who fled the country because of Vietnam and the several deaths some of our classmates. It's all there like the current under the deep river of history that we have become for each other. Is there anything to be gained in opening up those wounds. Will we simply meet with each other and have fun too and remember only the happy moments of our youth. That is likely to be the game plan. Bob's Storck says I must go, and if I do will I be once again the curious outsider, the middle class boy from Pennsylvania like Bob among my privileged classmates driving their Ferraris or Lamborghinis. I must, and travel all that way just to be a negative force is not worth it. What kind of 70th birthday present to myself will that be? After this summer, I should really retire and focus on my writing and not take on major projects. October should be a quiet or month. If the college won't plant a tree in Williams memory and let me sneak in the ashes as the tree is planted, I'll go one day to the lake in the Arboretum and pour small container of his ashes among the water lilies and he will fly off the wheel as Buddha has instructed, as will I, everything still a mystery.

4. DAPHNE

August 8, 2016

Dear Bob,

I'm happy to report that my cataract surgery went well and my vision is much improved, if not my Vision. The surgeon was little gay guy who wore blue socks and held both of my hands when we first met. He slicks his hair back like Batman or Spock in Startrek. But is a wizard in the operating room. Had me in and out in 10 minutes. I am a little claustrophobic, however, and when they strapped my head to the table to keep it from moving, I had to jump until the lovely valium kicked in. Now, I have only to put in drops throughout the day, and hope for continuing enlightenment.

The marathon birthday celebrations in August have me pre-occupied. Some weeks ago, I invited Brett Raphael for lunch at the suggestion of a friend. His mother worked with Margaret Mead and did important work for the UN on breast feeding in the third world. Brett is the founding director of the Connecticut Ballet and I came up with the idea of recreating the Daphne legend here at Riverrun. I envisioned a lithe dancer being chased by Apollo through the beautiful trees here. So, we are on now for this event and I spend my time trying to raise money to provide food and wine for the guests who will be coming. But in October, I plan to get my house in order and retire to the life of a writer – living more modestly, and not taking on any new projects. Well, that's my story and I'm sticking to it as my mother was fond of saying. Here is the lineup for the marathon weekend I have planned for later in the month. Wish you were here, and again, I am sorry. Love to you both. Richard

"Should I stay or should I go." There are two ways to approach birthdays that end in 0 – you either ignore them or you go for it. This August, my 70th on earth, I plan to go for it. Here are ways you can help me and friends celebrate. No presents please, just the present of your company during some nice events. Richard

AUGUST 17

POETRY READING WITH GRAY JACOBIK, JUDE RITTENHOUSE AND RICHARD HARTEIS

Join three celebrated poets for a reading and book signing. This event is free, and wine will be served!

**Savoy Bookshop & Café
Wednesday, 8/17
6 p.m.**

BOOKSHOP & CAFÉ
10 CANAL STREET, WESTERLY
401-213-3901
WWW.SAVOYBOOKSHOPCAFE.COM

AUGUST 20

DAPHNE: A SUMMER PLEASURE

The Connecticut Ballet (connecticutballet.org) and the William Meredith Foundation Invite you to a reenactment of the Daphne legend in an original dance and musical presentation at Riverrun, William Meredith's home on the Thames River featuring Katia Jirankova Levanti as Daphne and Harold Blackhood as Apollo. Staging by Brett Raphael, and music by Daniel Levanti. Because of her beauty, Daphne attracted the attention and ardor of the god Apollo. Apollo pursued her and just before being overtaken, Daphne pleaded to her father, the river god Landon for help. Landon then transformed Daphne into a laurel tree. Bring a lawn chair and be prepared for a very special afternoon. Complimentary wine, bread, cheese, fruit. Suggested donation $10 to benefit both foundations.

337 Kitemaug Road, Uncasville, Ct. 06382 – 3-5:30 p.m. 8/20/2016

R S V P : 860--961-5138 **WILLIAMMEREDITHFOUNDATION.ORG**

AUGUST 21

Courtyard Art Gallery

12 Water St. #B3

AUGUST 20 Mystic, Mystic, Ct.06355

RICHARD'S BIRTHDAY PARTY

SUNDAY SALON 3-6

READING

4:00   AND   CAKE!

860-536-5059

5. EMAIL CHAIN TO AN OLD FRIEND

I guess I will have to redact parts of this email chain and try to make sure it doesn't wind up in Hillary's email server, ha and ha. It has been good to be in touch with my old friend Bill this past week. Makes me sad though to think we are getting old now and must face the challenges of ageing. I remember the consolation William tried to give me when my dear pet, Astra was killed by a motorcycle when she was still in middle age, that she would not have to face the challenges of old age, the diminution of powers and health. I think too of my older brother Bob who is making a conscious effort to age with dignity and purpose and spirit. This is a good and important goal. I think too of poets like Richard Wilbur who has always been a gentleman and remains elegant and so solid spiritually despite the death of his wife and other trials he has faced in his life. We all get out alive perhaps, but living elegantly up till that moment is the goal.

Dear Bill,

I imagine you and Maggie are sore busy now that the election is in full swing. I have decided that I am "with her" because of the policies she espouses and out of great misgivings about Trump. But perhaps you will find a little time to participate in one of the events I have planned for a kind of marathon birthday celebration in August. I am feeling somewhat valedictory as I approach my 70th birthday – a time to take stock of where I've been and where I am going. Right now I am in the process of trying to raise the necessary funds to provide refreshments and wine for the guests we expect on August 20th for the DAPHNE program. I'm always at the edge it seems, and am faced with the task of providing for this event. The wine alone should cost about $250. If there is anyway you can help, it would be a great reading in Westerly should be good too. You would be able to meet Gray Jacobik who won this year's Meredith Award for Poetry. The Savoy is a new book store and café you may have already discovered.

I am fine, looking forward to Nancy's visit for a week to help me on these projects. I still dream of William a few times a week, reliving some dream failure on my part: This morning I left him in his wheel chair on the sidewalk and watched from the upper window as thugs patrolled the street looking for marks. Cynthia MacDonald told me once in such cases you simply have to get out of bed. Last week, I had cataract surgery, which one old lady calls Cadillac surgery. "If thy right eye offend thee…." as the Bible says. And I have started another book called reunion which will recount our class reunion in Switzerland in September. Bob Storck is underwriting this travel since he can't go. He has said I must report in a memoir, and so our little game of patron/artist. Perhaps I'll include one of the installments with this letter. Well, "back to my spuds," as Mrs. Lemington says in William's poem, "Roots." I hope you are both well and loving life as am I, and are full of expectation for what may come if Hillary does indeed take the White House. Love, Richard

Hello Richard

Good to hear from you and get the news. I'd be pleased to spring for the wine for the 20th and will send a check to Riverrun au matin. Your week of fetes is badly timed for us—we'll be in DC the first part of next week (Mag is a co-chair of Hillary's transition team—of course she'll need to win—and its initial meeting is Tues) then we head to the Vineyard where an old friend is letting us use a fine little house—Mag has been working hard at Harvard, and we went to convention which was work for her (look at Showtime's DNC episode of "The Circus" to see a rare Mag interview) and she needs a hideaway. We love the Savoy and all it adds to our little town—but you'll be back. Just turned 70 myself and celebrated by ignoring it. Since men our age must trade medical tales mine is the ablation I had a few weeks back; I'd hoped it'd quash my afib but it left some, but slowed it down.

Noble Barrett,

You have relieved a certain amount of stress in my life at the moment. Why do I take on these projects I wonder sometimes? I go from a simple little light bulb turning on imagining Daphne running through these trees, and suddenly the lawn is turned into a Fairgrounds. But it will all work out somehow, and your contribution will be a big help. I love you for that and for the moral support you continue to give to William's memory and the foundation. When you speak of the operation you mean an electro cardio version don't you? I had 3 of them over the years as I recall but the A-fib always came back. So, I rely on blood thinners to keep me healthy. Congratulations on your own birthday Bill. At 70 I'm thinking of what has gone before, and what may lie in store for the future. I met a fellow in Palm Beach who has a proposal in to grow medical marijuana. It's a big project and we'll know about mid August if they are awarded a a license by the state. If he wins, I've told him and the CEO I would move to Maryland and work on that project if a real salary were involved. Very interesting that Maggie is part of the transition team at this point. I'd make a very good bureaucrat. I'm loyal, verbal, and have all my marbles. I'm sure Maggie needs to hide out at this point. Probably every single person you know is looking to hire on. I'd make a very nice Ambassador to Bulgaria, for example. I'm a citizen there , and have a little bit of the language which could be brought up to speed. The second gay Ambassador in Europe, why not? But if not the top man, I could be part of that team for a while. Russia continues to make real inroads among the people as far as I can see and we have our work cut out for us there. Well, so much for the commercial. My dad always used to say all he wanted was ten more good ones and at 70, I think I can still hope for that too. Thank you again for the contribution. And I am serious about wishing to do some paying work in the future so I can keep this house and pay my bills. Everyone I know seems to have managed a lot better in terms of looking after their financial future. Well, it ain't over till it's over as the great Yogi says to which some wit added, yeah but when it's over, it's OVER. As is this missive which comes with love to you both.

    Richard

P.S. I'm about to have a little fun/gin right now as Chris Matthews comes on. Here is my resume, should lightning strike, by the way. Since everyone I know practically is a Leo with birthdays in August, I recall the letter Hillary kindly wrote for William's birthday party when she was First Lady:

"The arts have always been a unifying force in our world, bringing people together across vast cultural, social, economic and geographical divisions. Through his work, William Meredith both enhances and strengthens the American spirit. As you honor Mr. Meredith, you celebrate the timeless power of poetry and poets as our American memory, our purveyors of insight and culture, our eyes and ears who silence the white noise around us, and express the very heart of what connects us, plagues us, and makes us fully human."

Eugene Robinson says in an editorial today to fasten our seatbelts for what it sure to be an even dirtier campaign. Let's hope it is a landslide after what it likely to be a mudslide.

To: Bill Barrett

Ablation surgery. That's right, I remember it now. A couple of years back I was told I was a good candidate for it myself. But it seemed a bit experimental at the time. I did have another procedure a couple of years ago, ablation-wise: a carefully calculated radioactive pill to take out my thyroid. I bit the bullet as it were, or like Jack and the Beanstalk, swallowed the pill instead. Seems to have only half worked. Why aren't we sitting like two overly tanned old prunes on Miami Beach trading tales and complaining about our doctors? Or

Masquamicut Beach for that matter? I miss you brother. As my friend Helen said some years ago before she died, these days don't come back.

To: Richard Harteis

Send me your snail mail address please—I'm in NY and left my tattered old address book behind—and my memory don't work right. I gather ablations are pretty routine these days. They went up through my groin into the offending chamber and burned little rings around the guilty electrical tissue—evidently the scar tissue blocks the extra heartbeat signals—something like that. I was out for 6 hours and when I came to and the drugs wore off my heart hurt like hell. I hadn't signed up for that. A couple friends had ablations that totally wiped out the afib. Mine's maybe two-thirds gone. Ah the beach—I haven't been on our beach in two years—so much bouncing around—Cambridge NY DC RI. Hopefully heading for quieter times old friend.

To: Bill Barrett

It makes sense, doesn't it. You burn a muscle which is enervated and it is bound to hurt. I hope the pain is resolved by now and that you got some good pain medication post op. I remember all the broken bones, and lab tests and other sad challenges dear William had to face for decades. When I go through something successfully (like having my head strapped to the operating table for this cataract surgery, and me a major claustrophobe), I say to myself, "William is proud of me."

Sneak my resume into Maggie's briefcase. There is still a little life left.

6. CROSSING THE RUBICON

August 28, 2016

I have finally bought my tickets for Bulgaria, crossed the Rubicon. Lyubomir Levchev has arranged for me to spend a week at the Writers Union House in Sozopol and I have had to add a lot to my ticket to be able to return a week later. But, after much agonizing and advice from friends (baby sister in San Diego says "Nothing like travel," and Patrick says "go for it.") He invited me to go to mass with him this morning and we talked it over over brunch at Eileen's today. We had the entire summer to recoup our friendship, but it never seemed to happen — we have become "just friends" after two years of rehab for him and uncertainty for me of what is to become of us. But that is another story. It seemed silly to go to Bulgaria for just 4 days and so now I hope to finish this saga at the Black Sea as I did for the last book I did, WMD.

One bright idea I had yesterday was to carry William's remaining cremains to the Rila Monastery in the mountains outside of Blagoevgrad where I spent a year as Fulbrighter. We lived in the blok that year and it became our official home when we were made citizens of Bulgaia by presidential decree. That fall, we visited the blind soothsayer Vanga in Rupite and she and I seemed to have a telepathic conversation in which I asked her if I were to be buried in Bulgaria. Who knows, I may yet be. William had no problem with the idea. "What happens if you die here," I asked him once when he was just out of heart surgery and we debated on the wisdom of making the trip. "Well, I'll be buried here," he said.

The Episcopal minister I brought in when William actually was in the process of dying consoled us both. "Catholics can be cremated, but are not permitted to separate a person's ashes," I informed him. "Well, God is very powerful, and I imagine on the day of judgment he will be able to gather them all together for us to rise again." He was a sweet priest and his tongue in cheek admonition found a gentle response in me.

In the middle of my letter to the abbot, I get a call from Robert Storck who is playing Lorenzo de Medici by financing my trip to Switzerland. He says he has bad news and I am afraid he is going to ask for the money he has lent me back. Turns out he has fallen and had surgery on his quadriceps, a body cast in store for him for two months. We're at the age when old men begin to trade stories of their health. Our classmate, Bob Nish the beautiful red-headed boy from Phila has had his trouble too. Wife dead from cancer. But Bob will be at the reunion. He has two red-headed beautiful daughters at least. I wonder how he'll be, if that same sweet boyish smile will still be there. It is becoming difficult to see the loss that accumulates as I age among friends. How will Krassin be if he responds to this letter. I manage to include a photo of him and Blaga Dimitrova at the end of the letter to pull on his heart strings a bit. Beautiful Blaga, Updike's "Bulgarian Girl," who became the first vice president of Bulgaria after the change. And also a shot of Krassin at the Library of Congress visiting William and promoting Bulgarian poetry when Krassi was the Cultural Attache at the Bulgarian embassy.

"Blaga, what's up," I asked her in the late 80's as "the change" was about to take place against one of their brothers. Peter Manolov lay dying from a hunger strike after the police broke in and took all his writings.

"Aren't you afraid to be seen with me here in the lobby," I asked her.

"They know where I live, they know what think. My husband has been in interrogation now for 12 hours."

"Can I see the letter."

Our Ambassador was very glad to have the letter and know who was behind the velvet coup….

So, tickets finalized. What a return it will be. Will it be my last I wonder.

Dear Krassin,
I have thought of you often, though we seem not to be in frequent communication. I hope that is about to change. I have been copying you on various emails to keep you in the loop for upcoming travel. And it is my great hope that I can see you when I come and perhaps travel with you a bit. One goal I have is to go to Blagoevgrad and take the small (2 oz.) amount of William's remaining ashes and see if I can have them placed in the Rila Monastery. There would not be a need for a marker of any sort necessarily, but I would like to have a priest "officiate" with a prayer. I think this appropriate since we lived there and this is Bulgarian address of record. I think of the Irishman James David Bourchier who was such a supporter of Bulgarian culture and nationalism and who is buried in the region if not in the monastery itself. I would go to Blagoevgrad on the morning of the 21st of September and stop at the Monastery on the way, spending the night there. The following morning I

would need help getting a bus or transportation to Sozopol where I have been invited to spend a week at the Writer's Union House. I arrive at 10:00 pm on the 19th and will be staying in Sofia at the Rila Hotel the 19th and 20th. I hope to see Lyubomir who has not been well and who does not leave the house now apparently. Anyhow, I would be extremely grateful if you could contact the "archimandrite" of the monastery to see about such a visit on the 21st around lunch time en route from Sofia. From the internet I got the following information for contact: Info@Rilskimanastir.org. I will write an email to explain what I have in mind and ask his help, but you as the consummate diplomat and native Bulgarian and would probably add a lot to the prospect of it actually working. I hope this letter reaches you via email as well. I feel very nostalgic about this trip, somewhat valedictory. It may be my last to Bulgaria, I don't know. For now, I can only say many thanks. Here is a shot of you and Blaga I came across as I prepared for this trip. Now she is gone too and I wonder if anyone recorded her historic courage before she died….

Yours, Richard

Krassin Himmirski, First Bulgarian contact

7. RUSSIANS ARE GOOD WITH NOSTALGIA

Russians are good with nostalgia, that Russian soul: "surely all vanished now…."

Sat at the river, tiki lamps burning, the dog running like wildfire after deer, squirrel, what have you. The other day I went halfway down the steep stair to the point and saw her perched high on the highest point of rock overlooking the river. Incredibly dicey. She stood there like a mountain goat just staring at me across the railroad tracks, not showing off, just getting a better view of where I was. She tracks by sight, not smell so much. And she was like a laser on me. She is coming into her own now on the river. Something new for her genes I suppose—Australian Cattle Dog she. She has a dark devil intelligence about her and I don't think I've ever felt the combination of "otherness" of living with such an animal and the intimacy of living with an animal where you actually speak to each other. I guess they feed each other.

Well, will I resurrect this email chain and work it into something concise and interesting. One main issue in reading emails by tiki light on the river is to find Charlie Timberlake's email soliciting funds for his charity bike ride. He has had a real battle with throat cancer and is now riding for the cure. He gave us thousands in the beginning of the Meredith Foundation and I will send something in honor of the foundation. He is no longer a patron and I will not go to him having been chastised (Nancy insists on calling him Chaz—they developed a friendship after he bought thousands in sculptures from her. Charlie will be there with his wife, the former dancer Pat from New York. I do not wish to be chaztised once again. A nasty little pun, I can see this is going south and need to make some diner for myself. This is the kind of real reflection I make at what might be my more than late years. I just noticed that I have a nodule on my lung (5mm) lower left lobe looking at the results from a new ct scan. Clever Dr. Pasha. He averted his eyes when he handed me the report, not wishing to be hung as the bearer of bad news? Well, we will meet a lung woman from India when I get back and see where we are. This trip is becoming more and more valedictory. But I keep an eye on myself and seem to be paying my bills somehow for the moment.

This to Lisa Ritchie who wants me to have her new book translated and published in Bulgaria, an update on Krassin Himmirski.

He introduced Wm to Bulgaria, has been a friend for many years. We taught a translation course at the American University. He divorced Natalia. She took up with a journalist here when I brought her to the Lyman Allyn Museum for an exhibition we had there. She is out in the mid-west I believe teaching. She was a very good artist. I've asked him to join me if the archimandrite at the Rila Monastery approves the placing of some of William's ashes in the monastery. Long story.

Lyubomir seems to be in the late stages of Parkinson's and doesn't speak English in any case. The man I relied on for all translations including books died this summer. It was a great loss I hope to set up a translation prize in his honor. The question is who would publish the translation. A bilingual Edition might be possible but no one in the US would be overly interested in such a book. It would have to be sold in Bulgaria I think. I'll test the waters but I really won't be meeting with publishers at this point I want to finish a writing project my of my own catch up with friends in Varna and look after the monastery visit. But we shall see.

And Lisa to me:

Alas, friends and colleagues popping off or en route. A bilingual edition would only go in Bulgaria, but I did have a sort of audience there, stemming from 1979, surely all vanished now...

8. SEPTIC GARDEN

September 2, 2016

"Though I am still a strong swimmer, I can feel this channel widen as I swim."

"Who does not envy the young dead? Every year
the odds increase against accomplishment.
There is a thinning out, a dilution."

    From *English Accounts*, William Meredith

I've told Bob Storck I will come visit him when I get back from Bulgaria to look after him a bit post surgery. Poor guy fell and tore his quadriceps tendon and will be in a body cast for two months. I think of the cover of my surgery text book which has a picture of a Greek soldier performing surgery on a fallen comrade. Will I be up for it myself, I wonder?

Old men trading stories of their health, as Barrett says. I ought to be writing this from Miami Beach, all shrunken up like a prune. But the Black Sea will have to do.

Charlie Timberlake writes to thank me for the modest contribution to his 62 mile bike ride to support the cure for throat cancer. Seems he beat the bullet this past year with a thin scar running down the length of his neck—the impulse to give the finger to death, healthy. Three days later he will be in Switzerland with all the rest of us, eyeing each other up. Will be need name tags to identify each other?

The day before I leave for DC and Europe, I meet with a lung guy to see about a nodule which has been discovered on my lower left lobe. What story is in store for me, I wonder? I have faced the Big C a number of times in my life, fortunately, and have learned not to make too much of it until you see the actual writing on the wall: "Ain't over until its over," as the great Yogi says, to which someone added, "yes, but when it's over, it's OVER." These days, they can pretty much cure pain I guess, even psychiatric pain, and my future contributions will go to hospice care.

I've also learned that it is not a good idea to be talking about your health. It's like going around with a big Scarlet C on your chest and as long as you live, it will always be on the back of friends' minds when they meet you for coffee or a swim in their pool. "How's he doing, I wonder? I wonder if it's come back. How long he has, how long I have. It tolls for thee, it tolls for thee...." Dorthy Parker said it all:

Resumé

Razors pain you;
Rivers are damp;
Acids stain you;
And drugs cause cramp.
Guns aren't lawful;
Nooses give;
Gas smells awful; You
might as well live."

So, why have I brought it up now, I ask myself. What will the story be if this writing ever sees light of day? Is this just a little self-pitying self-indulgence? Maybe it will be a modest hook for a reader. Did he make it? How did he do? - No skipping to the end please. The larger question for every writer: is anyone going to read this? Why go to the trouble? Am I only like that Paleoindian daydreamer taking embers to the cave walls is Lascaux to say to the world, "Hey, I was here. I hunted these creatures and got a few. Here is what they looked like." I'll put a big red C on the cover of this account if it is ever published....

In grade school, the first assignment when school begins again: write two pages on what you did last summer. This gives a teacher a little breathing room and lets the kids do the work initially, takes the edge off of having to return from the beach or the Catskills to deal with the little rug rats. But in that case, it is an assignment and the little classmates have to sit there and listen to the essays without throwing spitballs or asking for a pass to go to the boy's room.

Before the summer began, I sat on the terrace giving lunch to Brett Raphael, the founding director of the Connecticut ballet. A mutual friend of his mother suggested we meet and as I admired his mother so, I decided I'd like to meet him. He wore her same gentle eyes, a little sad and questioning. On a lark, I suggested he choreograph a ballet to tell the story of Daphne, the nymph of Greek legend who was transformed into a Laurel tree as Apollo pursued her. To my surprise, he bought the idea and so began days of rehearsals, fund raising and preparing the grounds for an audience.

A sweet guy at Home Depot donated Tiki torches and sunflowers and shrubs to cover the septic bubbling up in the center of the yard for me to plant. And it worked! No smell rising when we did the laundry or flushed the toilets too often, and a permanent source of water and fertilizer to keep them flourishing. "Richard, those plants must love what they're getting," my neighbor Rita called over as I sprayed the anti6 deer concoction used to keep them from eating the flowers.

I designed a flyer and got a great article in the press about the event and sure enough, the evening in question, it did not rain and 75 people spread out in lawn chairs to watch DAPHNE. I read the lgend from Ovid, Katia and Harold worked their magic for the audience. Dan Potter rolled in as a 15 foot-high puppet of Pineus the river god king who transformed his daughter into Laurel. And to make up for the tensions which had arisen among cast and crew, danced right up to my lawnchair and presented me with a golden leaf.

It is, I guess, just another phase of one's life on earth, that post-70 rumination on how much longer do I have, how will I face it in the end. Courage, dignity, kicking and screaming? "Rage, rage against the dying of the light?" Have I prematurely entered Kubler Ross's fifth stage, or is this a kind of preemptive denial.

"Wise men at their end know dark is right,
Because their words had forked no lightning,"
and others "crying how bright
Their frail deeds might have danced in a green bay...."

An email comes this morning from a poet pushing 90 and yet a third manuscript for me to publish: "Of course ekphrasis and those who would read the book would know it has nothing to do with fracking." And ethereal Johnes, hawking his exploration of the boundaries between dream and non-dream realities,in his firstbook which I have recently published: FIRES ETERNAL MORNING, "the deliberate exploration of the uncharted islands, the tidal waves, andthe hidden shoals and depths of the subconscious."

And Gray Jacobik, archangel poet to whom I had the honor of presenting the William Meredith Award for Poetry. May my frail deeds yet dance in a green bay?

"They are beginning to fall like plums" William said when asked if anything would ever come of the research he did on the Romantic poets and their mentor, Trelawney. In the end there were only three which we gathered together as "English Accounts" in his book which won the National Book Award, EFFORT AT SPEECH. I always featured myself as young Shelley in those poems. William, like Trelawny scorching his hand as he drew Shelley's heart from the fire the day they cremated the dead sailor boy on the beach. "Dream is my element, Trelawney says, contemplating his own end, a far gentlier going out into that good night. And now I will carry his ashes to the Rila Monastery where the King's heart is kept, and soon William's ashes, all that remains of the truly great man who was the love of my life.

Trelawny's Dream

I.

Edward John Trelawny, who is imagined to speak the following lines in his late middle age, survived his friend Shelley by almost sixty years, and lies beside him in the Protestant Cemetery in Rome. He seems to have met no man or woman in a long life whom he could marvel at and love as he did Shelley. Trelawny had intended to convoy the poet and Edward Williams (and cabin boy, Charles Vivian) when they sailed the Ariel out of Leghorn into the storm that drowned them, but Lord Byron's yacht, which he was commanding, was detained at the last minute by port authorities. He cremated the remains of his friends, and recovered the little boat, which appeared to have been run down by a larger vessel, though the violent squall into which the Ariel disap-peared would have been enough to founder the keel-heavy boat which Trelawny himself had unwisely designed for the novice Shelley.

— W.M

> The dark illumination of a storm
> and water-noise, chuckling along the hull
> as the craft runs tight before it.
> Sometimes Shelley's laughter wakes me here,
> unafraid, as he was the day he dove
> into water for the first time, a wooded pool
> on the Arno, and lay like a conger eel
> on the bottom—'where truth lies,' he said—
> until I hauled him up.
> But oftener the dream insists on all,
> insists on retelling all.
> Ned Williams is the first
> to see the peril of the squall. His shout to
> lower sail scares the deck boy wide-eyed
> and cuts off Shelley's watery merriment.
> The big wind strokes the catboat like a kitten.
> Riding the slate-gray hillocks, she is dragged
> by the jib Ned Williams leaves to keep her
> head. The kitten knows the wind is a
> madman's hand
> and the bay a madman's lap. As she scuds
> helpless, only the cockney boy
> Charles Vivian and I, a dreamer and a child,

see the felucca loom abeam. Her wet lateen
ballooning in the squall, she cuts across
wind and seas in a wild tack, she is on us.
The beaked prow wrenches the little cabin
from the deck, tosses the poet slowly to the air—he
pockets his book, he waves to me and smiles—then
to his opposite element,
light going into darkness, gold into lead.
The felucca veers and passes, a glimpse of a face sly
with horror on her deck. I watch our brave sailor
boy stifle his cry of knowledge
as the boat takes fatal water, then Ned's stricken
face, scanning the basalt waves
for what will never be seen again except in dreams.
All this was a long time ago, I remember.
None of them was drowned except me
whom a commotion of years washes over.
They hail me from the dream, they call an old man to
come aboard, these youths on an azure bay.
The waters may keep the dead, as the earth may, and
fire and air. But dream is my element.
Though I am still a strong swimmer
I can feel this channel widen as I swim.

Trelawny at Sompting, 1879

    II.

Sometimes I dream about those two cauldrons—
the one at Port Louis wherein I placed
the ruby-spangled Arab with my heart.
After the oil and camphor and ambergris, the
dark smoke rose and I sprang forward,
falling on the sand so near the fire
my hands were burned; and the one I had forged
at Leghorn, the iron machine for Ned and
Shelley. Shelley's brain seethed and bubbled but
the heart would not burn—a bright flame
stroked and stroked it, occasioned by a liquid
still flowing from it,
and I took it in my hand to examine it,

after shrinking it in sea water, yet
it was still so hot as to burn my hand badly

The day before, Ned Williams' handkerchief,
whole silk beside his exhumed carrion,
made Byron say, 'The entrails of a worm
hold together longer than the potters' clay of
which man is made.' During the burning, he
swam far out to sea.
If I told Miss Taylor now
to leave the tea things and go gather faggots
and set them under my tub, I could rejoin them,
Zela, Arabian bird, and restless Shelley.

In the Protestant Cemetery

III.

How did their lives go out from those deaths,
Keats' at the foot of the Spanish Steps, Shelley's in
the wild wave, accepted on the beach at
Leghorn, frail heroes, riding for sixty years the
dreams of Severn and Trelawny. How did their
lives survive? Who does not envy the young dead?
Every year the odds increase against
accomplishment. There is a thinning out, a
dilution. The old are in desperate trouble. These
did not lose their models. The great old man Severn
was painting in Rome when Trelawny in Sussex
wrote to Clare, 'I have an icy cold bath every
morning and then go out with my shirtsleeves
tucked up and work in the garden.'
When they left that century it grew old.
Middle-aged people raised a subscription to
lay the old painter next to his young friend.
The adventurer followed, having lately written
a letter to Rome: 'In the year 1822 I purchased
a piece of land from the then Custodian—
I believe your father—under the pyramid
of Caius Cestius. I deposited the ashes of
my Friend Shelley in the one tomb and

the other I left for my ashes . . .'
We are parodies of boys and girls and we're aging. After
thirty who can think of himself except
as foully wronged, only the satiric overtones vary.
Judging ourselves harshly for natural losses,
we throw ourselves with less and less confidence
on the charity of our youth. We need good examples, we
need these two old men here under the cypresses.

9. LABOR DAY

September 5, 2016

Looks like I'll be going backward and forward in time now that I am home safely from Europe. But I am going to use chronology to pull this tale together since much of it now will be "emotion recollected in tranquility," is that how Wordsworth described it? As I approached departure date for Switzerland, Labor Day loomed on the horizon, and life was interrupted by a skunk which got my dog and set me to thinking as fall began to announce itself.

What was that anecdote my literature teacher told about Wordsworth. Mr. Dorance, that was his name. Seems young Keats went to see the great man and presented him with a copy of his book. In those days you had to cut the pages yourself as you read the book since they were published in folios apparently. Years later they found Keats' book in Wordsworth's library and discovered it had never been opened by Wordsworth, the pages had never been cut, which led Mr. Dorance to describe it as the unkindest uncut in all of literary history. Ha ha.

So, now that the leaves have turned orange and time has marched on, I can only tip in the poem I wrote that day in September.

> I   Sprayed
> (with apologies to Rita and Pepé Le Pew)

> She's saved her sovereignty,
> But lost her virginity, skunk-wise.
> She is now not a dog with whom
> You would wish to nuzzle.

It didn't take an arsenal, just one bad actor
Placed strategically like an A bomb under
The neighbor's deck and my puppy's gone
Radioactive. I'd best bathe her before her
exquisite sense of smell drives her crazy
the way it's doing me, before the stink
permeates permanently throughout the house
Like summer road kill. And hope she's learned
the black-and-white-stripped one is not a kitten
to mess with. Time will need to cure this wound.

No amount of burning incense or Fabreze will
cover the rancid peanut butter smell rising like
a green gas from her bedding. It's going to
take gallons of tomato juice and oatmeal
shampoo to bring my sweet, penitent baby back
to me, so we can have breakfast and play ball.

II Wood Rot

My Paul Bunyan tenant has Glousterd out
The glass-green eyeballs from the plastic Owl
I have set up to keep the wood peckers
From attacking the house. He needed them
For his own craft creation, some kind of ogre
In driftwood hiding under a bridge lit up with
Christmas lights. Woody and his fellow peckers
are no longer scared of the blind bird meant to
threaten them away and guard the upper WC
wall where I am taking my morning constitutional.

Ho-ho-ho ho ho! Ho-ho-ho ho ho!
The wood pecker taps away like some
inspired jazz percussionist and no amount
of banging on the wall sends him away.
Daddy-longlegs have begun to make their
Slow march over the computer and book case.
Squirrels are beginning to put in a supply of
Acorns, and a scout bat wings in on occasion
To see if this might be a good place to roost.
Creatures are taking over now that fall has come,
And I sit here like so much wood rot, waiting
For the rains to come and later, snow.

10. Letter to Mikey

Dear Mikey,

Late at night I am drafting a letter with information on Sydney's care.

I will try to get a key made for the library tomorrow so you can visit here on occasion and let her run the grounds and come back into the library which is like her second home. She will feel comfortable. Walk to the point and she will follow you. Take a ball or toy to get her up to the house. Only you and your girlfriend are permitted to enter into the library please.

Always have water in the car and keep the windows open if it is getting hot. It gets hot very quickly in a car.

The nice guy we met at Sydney's vet is Dr. Bush. He is off exit 28 off
route 2 West I believe: Colchester Veterinary Hospital, LLC
Old Colchester Road, Colchester, Ct. 06415
Telephone: 860--537-3168

This letter will authorize you to seek care for her if needed.

She has been chipped and that is the yellow tag. I will get her number and put it in here.

I'll bring her metal bowls. She tends to get her color caught in the carriage for the bowels so I am just bringing the bowls. And her food. There should be enough for a two cups a day till I get back. If not, her diet can be ordered through Chewy (see attached) I will re-imburse you if you are running low and need to order. The second small bag is low in protein, but the chewy diet is best.

I'll bring her Emotional Support documentation, vest, and leash. In theory she can go anywhere like a service dog, but don't force it. Don't just assume she can go into a restaurant. If she is on a deck or outdoors, that would be more logical. Some people take offense at having a dog in their dinning area.

I can't think of anything else at the moment except to thank you from the bottom of my heart. You know how much this dog means to me. She is like a teenager and very willful and needs some discipline, especially is she begins to run free and is in an area she doesn't know and so would be tempted to try her wings and get lost, or run over by a car. Do your best buddy, I know you will. And enjoy the little bitch. She is exquisite and a blessing to us all. Richard

11. Met at Geneva

September 16, 2016

Well it was bound to happen at some point. Working with an iPad and cell phone, transferring back and forth because this year there is no wifi in the Union's apartment and so I must transfer back and forth when I am at the beach. All of yesterday's work is lost. Could it be a terrorist hack job, or just sloppy thinking after last night indulgence in pot which Bobo gave me as a little gift before I left Sofia? I recall that Hemingway lost an entire suitcase of his work traveling on the train which was really a loss for literature. Mine hardly qualifies for even a mention in comparison. And in the end, I can pick up the pieces another time. I just have to get back on the horse, but I don't have the heart to return to yesterday's work just now. And I say a prayer to St. Anthony, I might just be able to resurrect it from the trash when I get to beach and get on the internet again. But I do want to tell the tale in something of a chronological way and this is precisely why I blocked out this time in Sozopol to get it all down before the details begin to fade for me.

The morning of my departure, I woke with classic diarrhea – cause unknown. I had nightmare visions of loosing control of my bowels or bladder on the plane and so took a Flomax and went to the pharmacy to buy a kings portion of Lomotil. I kept this little drama from Nancy as she dropped me at Dulles on the 16 right on target: Kiss and Fly. I managed to pack and kiss the dog on the nose and set off. At the airport, suddenly the vest I had hanging on my suitcase disappeared, but thankfully it had no money or passport or some such. Amazing how fast that happened. I just turned around and suddenly it was gone. You kind of had to be there as the expression goes.

I wonder if such detail will really interest a reader. I remember how my English teacher took the Romantics to task for producing every detail of their lives, the laundry bills, what they ate, the weather. Maureen O'Brien thanked me for the entry in "my journal" in one email. Is she pointing out that a journal is not a memoir? What could be the dramatic hook in this piece at this point unless the reader skips to the end and we discover that Hillary Clinton did or did not make it to the presidency. That I have lung cancer, bladder cancer, the need of a new hip? This has become something of a memoir inside a memoir since I've had to return to my notes to fill in the final details of the Swiss reunion.

I remember meeting a sweet guy from Iran on the plane going over. He was circumspect as we chatted, but after a number of hours we got to know each other the way strangers do, and it was quite moving. He was an engineer and apparently had dual citizenship because he traveled back and forth routinely. A brother in the states had cancer and he had returned to look after him. He was not married, but my gaydar didn't pick up any particular vibe in that regard. As we got into the flight he turned out that his primary interest in life was mysticism and he was quite familiar with new age writers. I was amazed at the writers he knew such as Tolle and certain Indian mystics. I was the up front American, hail fellow, well met. He was the distinguished Iranian, formal, careful in his language and thinking.

"Are you really planning to build a nuclear weapon," I asked him.

"I haven't seen anything like this in public and the nuclear watchdogs are everywhere in the country. I guess you can only go by what you see."

I told him of my anxiety about the long flight and how sorry I was to be stuck in the middle seat and needing to disturb him all the time. Either because the seat was so tiny (or me too big!) or I was reacting to all that Momotil and Flowmax, I was having a little trouble breathing.

"Are you all right," he asked me. And it was clear he was going to keep an eye on me throughout the flight, a regular Good Samaritan. Nice. Did he have these sensitivities from looking after his brother. What an elegant fellow. Mysterious. But elegant. It was nice knowing he was sitting beside me and concerned for my health. An Iranian! Suck it up Donald Trump.

The last book I wrote, a memoir titled WMD memoir was similar project to this after I discovered I had White Matter Disease in 2013. I decided that if I were going to loose my mind and personality, I might as well write about it for the sake of other "boomers" coming along who might benefit from my own history. Lou Gehrig's Disease, MS, Parkinson's, or just a "harmless sign of aging." But it turned out not to be so grave. My sweet neurologist, Dr. Smith has danced around the subject and not given me a diagnosis, which is okay by me. We just do an annual MRI and monitor the progression. I imagine if there were an appropriate medication for whatever he suspects I have, I would be on it by now. Whatever it is, it seems close enough in the Medicare classifications for him to prescribe medical Marijuana. So, there is some benefit at least. By the time I get back to the US, my new license will be in the mail - Unlike Bond's license to kill, I have a license to live.

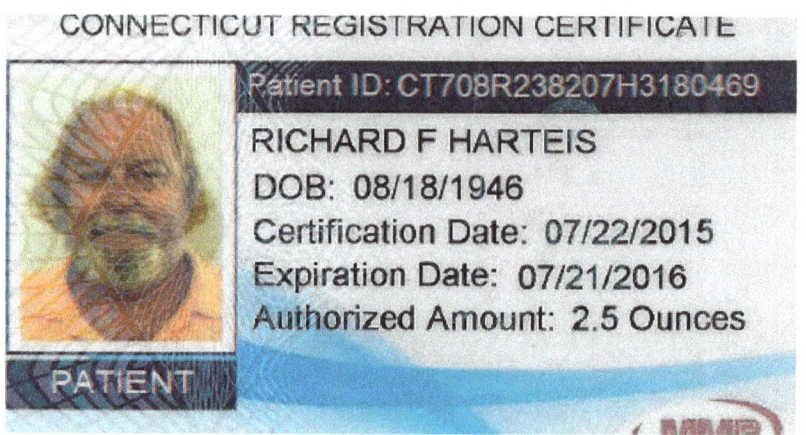

When I arrived in Geneva, there was sweet Judy Cole waiting to meet me, a sight for sore eyes as the say. In fact my recent cataract surgery was a bit painful and the chronic dry eye as well.

When I worked as the health officer in a Westinghouse project in Morocco – building a state of the art air traffic control System of the Royal Moroccan Air Force, Judy was working in Rabat on an NGO project to help improve the lives of women through small economic development projects. She was an attractive divorcee with a couple of kids and several men on our team were interested in her. One was a young, hot-dog engineer named Jerry, who I sometimes traveled with into the desert to meet our men for medical call. "What these boys don't understand, " the HR guy from Alabama, my boss, told me "is that they are living in a Kingdom. Look around. Everything you see here belongs to the King. I mean he's the KING, man. They can't just go out and get some girl pregnant and let the court decide who the daddy is. The local chief is going to cut off their head or something worse if they don't just marry the girl."

Another team member, an upper level manager named Ray was also after her and in the end she chose Ray. She had the luxury of going back to law school and parlayed her degree to a high level position with the UN in Geneva in charge of refugees. After some decades, she chose to stay in Switzerland and Ray retuned to Baltimore where his grandkids from a previous marriage were growing up. Like many a marriage between ambassador and spouse, they remained committed and kept up their marriage and affection for each other long distance. So, she had flourished and was now savvy as a native about train schedules, local customs, and the international agencies ringing the Lake in Geneva.

There she stood as I got off the plane in the middle of what seemed like an upscale shopping mall which is the airport in Geneva. The connections flight from Frankfurt was a nightmare of conveyor belts, stairs and escalators. "Are you sure you want to buy your duty free here," the girl at the counter asked. "It is a lot of walking."

"No, I'll be fine I said, "showing off my brand new cranberry suitcase and how easily it rolled on all four wheels. Little did I know she was talking about *kilometers* of travel before we even got to the bus carrying us to the plane. It was an enormous operation, building after building off in the distance.

A nice young guy from Belgium who offered me his seat, looked out at the sprawling mess as though he were looking at Oz. "It gives you joy, doesn't it," I asked him. His face was radiant. "Ya, it's awesome."

"I'd call it disgusting," I said breathing hard, my shirt soaked with sweat. "It's not designed for human beings." The boy just smiled, and I regretted coming off like a disgruntled old codger as he gaped at the brave new world he would inherit.

Geneva was more to order. Judy pointed out the escalator going down to the trains and helped me purchase a ticket at the self-serve machines for my travel to Fribourg. Then off we went for a little tour of her town in the suburbs along the lake shore.

She was very proud to show me one building after another housing NGO's, UN embassies and various international organizations where she had worked. The real work of the "UN is done here," she said. "New York is just a show place." Though retired, she took pride in the work she did helping the refugees of the world.

We passed the famous "broken chair," a enormous sculpture symbolizing the plight of refugees and the world's response or lack of response to their dire circumstances.

I had the wit not to deride what I considered a corrupt institution which enabled third rate diplomats from poor countries to live high on the hog and use their diplomatic immunity to behave badly and even cover up the occasional serious espionage. I was a kind of refugee myself, and her desire to help me was heartfelt. She took great pride in the village of Coppet where Madame de Staël wrote her best-selling pot boilers and held forth entertaining the likes of Mozart and anti-Napoleon revolutionaries at the salons she held at her Chateau.

All so picture perfect, so Swiss: the blue and white shutters indicating a government building, the sing song courtesy of the girl at the pastry shop, flower boxes at every corner right on down to the lake side.

But the country still has one of the highest suicide rates in Europe. More suicides are committed here using guns per capita than anywhere else in Europe. I've heard this fact blamed on den Fern, the low pressure system that caused all sorts of psychological havoc, a similar excuse as the Mistral in France, winds blowing up from Africa.

More likely, having to live up to the standard of perfection at every level had more to do with it. Wound tight like so many watches, the young people had so many expectations to live up to. And in the silence of those perfect winters the silence and pressure worked on you. I remember sitting at my desk as a student there, meditating on the art of Francis Bacon, letting the liquid flesh of his models terrify me, taking over my own spirit. You could understand how Frankenstein was born there across the lake in the mind of Mary Shelley. You longed to get to France or Italy where things were a little messier. A nice country, but, yes you might have second thoughts about wanting to live there.

It certainly suited Judy just fine. A golden parachute and small inheritance had enabled her to buy an exquisite apartment outside the village behind "her" vineyard which apparently was protected by law to remain as long as grapes were grown. She gave me lunch and we caught up for an hour before she put me on the train at Noney and off I went to the reunion adventure.

With a change in Lausanne, I was able to get to the hotel in time for a nap and the first of the scheduled reunion dinners. These were to be our main activities and I wanted to be alert despite the enervating jet lag. The perfect views of the lake and exquisitely groomed countryside with corn fields planted in postage sized fields were seductive despite the dramatically overcast skies over the lake and I nodded off to the rhythm of the train until mellifluous voice of the robot lady announced the arrival in Fribourg.

12. PROVINCETOWN

A year ago, I was having my hearing checked and as incentive to come in, clients were offered a two-day holiday for free. There were all sorts of restrictions, of course, penalties if you changed the reservation, pages of small print caveats. But I was determined to try it out and sure enough spent the last two days in Provincetown, a rather nostalgic end of summer break from the books in the pipeline I hope to publish before Christmas. One of them is to be this reunion account, in fact, and I had thought to make it a working vacation.

In my Proustian mind's eye, I was to re-magine the flight to Switzerland and the three days spent with classmates at our reunion and then on to Bulgaria. So, this must be a little side entry out of synch with that account since it prepares me for what will be the final reunion coming up next weekend.

My main touristic goal for this vacation was to attend the Sunday afternoon tea dance at the mega gay bar on the strip. When William died, I went to P town with a local friend who wanted to support me in my grief. I fell apart routinely during that time and he felt I had to get out and away. So, a stop at the tea dance was high on the list of summer fun in P town. By the time I checked into the hotel and got to the the bar, the party had pretty much ended and I had a lonely solitary cocktail before walking the streets to buy some salt water taffy and see what the end of summer looked like.

The air was chilly, fall had already come. Many of the stores had Halloween decorations up and people still crowded the streets though they were bundled up in scarves and hoodies. I came across one gallery that featured a giant rabbit in the window, but peeking from behind was a portrait of Hillary Clinton. By the time this journal is ended, we will know if she actually made it to the White House. Next weekend I may meet my friend Barrett's wife Maggie who is co-chair of the transition team for Hillary at a brunch with my old Peace Corps buddy, Roger who is visiting from Seattle. This will be the final reunion of my season of reunions and will have to be the last chapter if this book is to see light of day in 2016.

Barrett lived across the hall from William when William was the US Poet Laureate. I was working in Morocco and so Barrett profited from William's friendship those two years with invitations to the Library of Congress and social life in DC. When Barrett married Margaret, William and I were their guests at the wedding and I left in plenty of time to find handicapped parking at Trinity Chapel. As we pulled into the university I saw a character up ahead in a cap and wearing sweats who I thought could give me directions. We only had a half hour to be there on time.

When I pulled up to the person I thought was a maintenance man, it turned out to be Margaret.

"My God Margaret, you're going to get married in a half hour and look at you!"

"I thought I'd dress down," she said and laughed.

A half hour later she floated down the aisle in a gray silk bare-shouldered gown with a train 20 feet long. Spectacular. More beautiful than Dianna Ross, more stylish than Aretha Franklin. Bill Clinton came in wearing crutches from some mishap with a golfing buddy along with Hillary too. And they were seated *behind* me and William. HA HA.

Margaret, Hillary's intimate from the earliest days has continued to play an éminence grise over the years but managed to stay well in the shadows. She is a genuine friend and can shake Hillary by the shoulders and tell her to wake up when needed. "Margaret, why did she stay with him through all that Monica stuff," I asked her once. "She loves him," Margaret reported. It was as simple as that. And I knew it was true.

Mike Fitzgerald was the prime mover to organize the reunion and make it a reality. Here he is along with his wife Marilyn at the Georgetown reception. And I can thank Marilyn for the good photo of me and Nancy Frankel, my sweet date for the party.

At the 40th Georgetown Reunion, William had just died and I was a wreck. I decided to drive to Wilmington anyhow and the enormity of my loss struck me as I drove through the beauty of summer. We had a mass given by Father Bodner, the chaperone/tour guide/and travelling companion who accompanied us to Fribourg. His compassion for my loss and that of all the others in attendance were crucial in that initial period. By the 45 reunion, Father Bodner had passed away and part of the reunion became a celebration of his life.

I was anxious to get Bill's Barrett's take on how things were going in the election, since Margaret was now co-chair of Hillary's transition team. And so, after all this shameless name dropping (I wonder if we will remain friends if this is ever published) we made a date to meet Roger and Barrett for lunch and yet another reunion in the summer of reunions.

Lunch at the Pink Basil

We thought the Steak Loft at first, but it was such a beautiful day we decided on the Thai place at the back of the shopping center. Good food and a terrace where they would provide a water dish for Sydney, my Emotional Support Animal. Two answers to people who ask why I have the gall to bring a dog to a restaurant terrace: She keeps me social and I feed her, or with her I keep from killing people who confront me about my dog. Very pleasant at the Pink Basil. No reply necessary. Next table over, two beautiful small girls just back from the Aquarium with their mothers playing with the Sea Horse stuffed toy souvenirs who were charmed by having a dog next door.

Roger surprised us by inviting Don Werner, an old New Haven friend of theirs who came looking like the spirit of Halloween. He hasn't convinced the VA that all his cancers are a result of agent orange from his Viet Nam service. When he and Roger get together, Roger calls it the organ recital. Don had just lost a lung after throat cancer and hasn't had solid food for 15 years.

"You're a hero, Don," I kept telling him. I couldn't believe the good humor he had through it all. Skeleton thin, with a new set of dentures that gave him a grim reaper smile, he joked about the VA and said how pissed off he was that his friends were all making $1200 a month disability and he didn't get a penny. We all sat in front of mounds of Pad Thai and he had a Coke. What people put up with.

Barrett too had just had an ablation of his heart which apparently didn't take and requires a second shot. No one had filled him in on the pain after this procedure when they burn out that portion of the heart that initiates the haywire electrical circuitry causing a-fibrillation. Roger was able to one up him with his tale of a pacemaker out of whack going off eight times in three hours until the battery got fixed.

We drank our Shingha Beer and munched on spring rolls. Seems I have beat the bullet lung-wise and bladder-wise after a series of MRI's. But the latest wrinkle is a hip joint out of kilter – Will find out tomorrow what my bone guy has in mind for me. Meanwhile, good old Dr. Smith has re-uped my medical marijuana license for another year. No MRI change there. He won't tell me what he thinks I have, he'll only give me the Medicare code that enables me to charge for his care. It's a little game between us. I don't want to know any more than he wants to get into it. With my penchant for rumination, it's just as well I carry on in ignorance. When I start falling down and crying without reason, it will be time enough.

And that may come sooner than I think depending on what happens in the election in a week. Would I really go to Bulgaria or Canada to live if America got Trumped? My email to Bill will not, I hope, find its way in the FBI. With Trump as president all bets are off.

I'm very happy we caught up with you yesterday. Wonderful to be there with you and Don and Roger. I hope my dog wasn't too much of a problem with her kelping. We don't want to prejudice you and Maggie against the idea of a dog in your life. And thank you again for paying for lunch. You are such a generous soul. Your buying the wine for Daphne was another example of your friendship to William and me. I'll send a little dvd of the ballet that we did by way of thanks.

Here are some shots of the boys at lunch. And one of the Queen looking very fly. As Donald Trump might say, "I'd do her." I think it will be ok for Hillary, though I would fire Comey's ass when she gets into the White House or at least bring him up on charges if she doesn't have that power. It could have made a real difference I think in the congress if this hadn't come up. But there is no putting the milk back into the bottle I guess. We just have to hang on for another week. Don't forget, I want to be Ambassador to Bulgaria. I'll write again from Sofia. Love, Richard and Sydney

And Bill writes back in part:

"We're pretty optimistic about Hillary though it is possible it'll be taken from her. At the least, Comey has very much diminished her having a friendly Senate-ifshewinsbuthasbothhousesagainstherit'llbeterrible,although she has a propensity for cutting deals with Repubs and could surprise. Mag & just want it over."

To which I say, God save the Queen and us all.

13. STING IS IN TUSCANY

"Sting is in Tuscany." This is how Entertainment Tonight describes the long silences between albums until suddenly a new masterpiece appears. I imagine him in his villa there, working at peace, eating well, contemplating cultures and music and seeing about something new.

I try to think of Riverrun, William's home on the Thames here in Uncasville as my Tuscany. I walked the dog to the secret garden where I have placed some of William's ashes under the remarkable tree that he wrote of. Fall now, and the deer have begun to eat the fancy Japanese maples and ornamental trees planted there. The angel baby statue stands grieving, Sydney is happy to chase a ball I throw to her, I close my eyes and try to feel his presence once more, hear his answer to the questions I pose.

A Couple of Trees

The two oaks lean apart for light.
They aren't as strong as lone oaks
but in a wind they give each other lee.
Daily since I cleared them I can see
them, tempting to chain saw and ax—
two hardwoods, leaning like that for light.
A hurricane tore through the state one night,
picking up roof and hen-house, boat and dock.
Those two stood: leafless, twigless, giving lee.
Last summer ugly slugs unleafed the trees.
Environmental kids wrote Gypsy Moths Suck.
The V of naked oaks leaned to the light
for a few weeks, then put out slight
second leaves, scar tissue pale as bracts,
bandaged comrades, lending each other lee.
How perilous in one another's V
our lives are, yoked in this yoke:
two men, leaning apart for light,
but in a wind who give each other lee.

I have to admit it has become a little boring night after night listening to MSNBC's blow by blow of who is ahead in the polls, the latest scandal. I've become obsessed by it, and depressed every time I listen to Trump's talking points ripping Clinton apart. Yesterday, Lawrence O'Donnel revealed that Melania Trump worked for pay while on a tourist visa and broke the law. "Oh no, she only worked Pro Bono," I posted on Facebook. I couldn't resist. But the post immediately disappeared. Seems I couldn't slide the little play on words past the Trump monitors at Facebook. RIGGED SYSTEM!

So, I will print this "journal" before Christmas or not at all, and just keep at it here in Tuscany. Not easy to remember the details of the final reunion – I was too taken up with reuniting to keep notes. So, I have to rely on photos to trigger my failing memory. WMD strikes again.

September 16, Reunion Dinner

As I rolled my new red suitcase down the road from the train station in Fribourg, I could see I was being eyed up by a not-too-savory looking character. A white guy, not a Muslim, but I thought of the recent stabbings on the trains in Europe and how un-Swiss to see someone who was obviously down and out in Switzerland. I checked into the very fancy NH Hotel where most of the reunites were staying, unpacked and crashed. When I came into the lobby several hours later, there they all were, about to stroll to the Café du Midi for fondue and my first night of the party.

The reunion was spread over two weeks, so I missed classmates who came earlier in the week. But I seem to have selected the primary weekend for the bulk of the classmates, at least the ones I remembered most. How could I forget Maureen O'Brien (second from left) who was the back up singer for our jug band. Spunky little Maureen, jumping up and down at my side like Minnie Mouse as we rocked the Aula Magna in a concert to raise money for the Israeli students who had to get back to Tel Aviv quick in the three day war. They were a couple of years older, med students, but also tank commanders who needed to get home in a hurry. The concert raised $25K, enough money to rent a Suisse Air flight day two of the war.

The two beauties dead center, Lynn Troy and Kathy Toborg hadn't changed much and revived the old chemistry as the evening started.

THE GIRLS

Mary Jo   Michèle   Lynn   Kathy   Maureen   Jan

THE BOYS

The boys, however, sustained the ageing process less well on a scale that went from no change (Bill Wisnewski) to various degrees of gray hair, paunch, and baldness.

John   Ed Charlie Bob Bill   Mike   Rich   Bill

THE SPOUSES

Jennifer   Gwen   Marilyn   Anne Mona Rob Pat   Klaus

These black and white photos from 1967 in Fribourg give you a sense of the before and after. John Carr is the hairy-chested guy in the upper right, the in-shape teenager below him is me with my English girlfriend, Alexandra Wood. Left of that, dramatic at my desk is Richie in black, trying to look like a Russian prince. Above that, me and John Carr visiting Rudy Van Sassen at his family's summer home in the Zeider Sea in Holland where we had gone sailing. Like all teenagers I sported a beard to make me look older and now sport to make me look distinguished possibly?

"A good time was had by all" as these pictures show, but what they don't show is the love for each other that flowed as freely as the wine at the tables as we broke bread together and dipped it into a pot of boiling Gruyere and Emmental cheese. Each of us had achieved varying levels of accomplishment (our zillionaire classmate, Doug Casey didn't make it to the reunion) but these friends all had earned some status in life that had nothing to do with money.

One continued years later looking after a husband in a wheel chair, another had beat cancer in a major way, a career in banking that took him for years to Japan where he became so enamored of the culture he built his own tea ceremony house. Beautiful Lynn had become gay, like me I guess, living with her partner in Vermont. She radiated such competence and compassion, and good will. The closest thing I can think to describe how I felt at dinner with these lovely folks is the James Wright poem, the Blessing which I will include here if I can get the right to reproduce it.

A Blessing
      by James Arlington Wright

Just off the highway to Rochester, Minnesota,
Twilight bounds softly forth on the grass.
And the eyes of those two Indian ponies
Darken with kindness.
They have come gladly out of the willows
To welcome my friend and me.
We step over the barbed wire into the pasture
Where they have been grazing all day, alone.
They ripple tensely, they can hardly contain their happiness
That we have come.
They bow shyly as wet swans. They love each other.
There is no loneliness like theirs.
At home once more, they begin munching the young tufts of spring
in the darkness.
I would like to hold the slenderer one in my arms,
For she has walked over to me
And nuzzled my left hand.
She is black and white,
Her mane falls wild on her forehead,
And the light breeze moves me to caress her long ear
That is delicate as the skin over a girl's wrist.
Suddenly I realize
That if I stepped out of my body I would break
Into blossom.

A toast to Mike Fitzgerald and Kathy (Wessels) Cook (below) who organized the reunion.

14. DAY TRIP

I've always liked this newspaper photo of William looking like a little Dutch boy from the studio bathroom window where the woodpecker is trying to peck out a home. This morning as I had my shower, the country western song came on in the shower radio: "I'll always have you to hold, That's all I need to know." But I no longer have him to hold, that's what I know now. And it set me crying a little. Mum too. Gone. My two best friends.

I decided to go to church before diving back into my account of Switzerland. From the pulpit, not a word about the election, the need to vote. The Bishop turned up and they celebrated veterans day instead, and the year of the submarine here in Connecticut. I imagine half the congregation will be voting for Trump, so a safer bet to celebrate the military. Every branch as represented and the full regalia of pipers from around the community in kilts and flags and drums. I tried to pray for some respite in my loneliness for William, some sense of spiritual peace or certainty which have escaped me for decades. But I was pre-occupied by a beautiful guy taking photos who looked like a young Tom Cruise. I guess young people have gone to church for centuries to meet other young people. But I don't imagine the Bishop would approve of this use of the Sunday Mass for gay guys. As I left the church, I couldn't resist asking the Bishop to say a prayer for Hillary as I shook hands. He laughed a little, a charming Bishop smile, but I couldn't help thinking of Pius XII's neutrality as the Nazi party began to flourish in Germany.

"No surprise in the writer, no surprise in the reader" Frost used to counsel debutant writers. I wonder if I'll find something surprising about day two of our reunion in Switzerland. Today is day two of the weekend leading up to the election. The surprise today is that Comey finds nothing more to prosecute from the emails found on Huma Abedine's computer.

I tried posting a couple of images from facebook side by side, sort of the before and after one is hoping for on election day. Let's cart him off to the dustbin of history, or at least not give him a permanent media forum for his bile. But Facebook would not let me post the two images. They seem to have very good monitors. Let's hope they do as well with ISIS and its recruitment efforts.

BEFORE   AFTER

The surprise of day two at the Château de Gruyères was missing my ride home at the end of the day. I don't recall ever visiting the castle when I was in Fribourg, so this was to be a real touristic adventure, a walk through eight centuries of architecture, history and culture. Seems twenty different counts held sway over the place between the 11th and 16th centuries. The last of them, Michel went bankrupt in 1554 His creditors, the cantons of Fribourg and Bern shared his earldom between them and in 1938 the chateau was turned into a museum.

Things started off well enough. Charlie had rented a car and invited me to join him and Pat on the trip to join our classmates on an excursion to the famous castle. Overcast and spitting rain like so many of the late fall days of our junior year abroad, the trip was nevertheless friendly as Charlie followed the GPS instructions coming from the dashboard.

"This country has too many damn roundabouts," he complained. But it was nice just to catch up and take in the beautiful countryside. As we got closer, like a scene out of The Sound of Music, all the traffic had to pull over at the ceremonial herding of the cattle being brought down from the mountains for the winter. The cows wore enormous bells and great garlands of wildflowers. Flowers everywhere, on the sheep, goats, cowboys, cowgirls. Everyone had to have a selfie with the parade.

Pat Timberlake was delighted by the detour. Pat and I were the slow pokes of the group, always drifting off to another room or lingering too long in the Burgundian Room oogling the capes of the Golden Fleece or the tapestries in Room of the Beautiful Lucy. Pat was a Rockette in the old days, something of a Beautiful Lucy herself and the beat goes on as the song says. I sensed just a hint of insecurity, she as the younger spouse in a group of people she didn't quite know how to read for the sake of their shared history together which didn't include her. Me, without a spouse always pushing me to be on time, or forget about shopping for chocolate till later, or put on your makeup in the car, we're running late, was a good gay side kick as we drifted through the castle, someone to make comments to, share an interest in the fancy silverware, the coat of arms of the Python family flanked by two angels, the small statue of Saint Sebastien meant to protect against the plague. Two middle class Ameri-can Catholics in the heart of protestant Europe.

This rather blurry shot I have included for the sake of the handsome cowboy in the black hat poking his head up over the black bossie in the rear.

We made our way up Esplanade to the Courtyard pretty much in unison like a Japanese tour group. A chance to take a snap of the pretty church at the bottom of the hill.

A choral group dressed in local costumes sang an acappella yodeling concert. And part of the village below the castle had become part of a bike race. Little girls offered the bikers pieces of banana and orange juice to keep their energy up. The streets were lined with cafes and stores selling chocolate and cheese.

But once inside the castle, we began to drift in different directions following our tastes. I liked the Hunting Room with all the stag horns gracing the walls, de rigeur for a real castle which is why every home in western Pennsylvania has last year's trophy hanging on the wall. The boys always went along to the hunting cabin with their uncles when it was time for deer hunting or turkey. When the Jack Daniels was finished and the fire had died down, you couldn't count on the uncles to take you outside for a pee. Too much snow, too cold to look after the rug rats sleeping in the bunk beds. Worse came to worse, a handy plastic tube ran outside the window and could be used as a urinal for the kid who had the top bunk, if he wasn't too shy to use it.

Tapestry in the Room of the Beautiful Lucy (Alexander's Victory? Ulysses meets Hector in front of the city of Troy?)

Pat in the Knight's room admiring the furniture of Auguste Ansermot from the end of the 19th Century.

My favorite room in the castle was the "Fantastic Art Room." The above painting of Pandora reminded me so much of Stoimen Stoilov's work, the Bulgarian master who I visit in Varna at the end of this reunion summer. All of the European traditions are clear in his work and in many of the surrealistic, Bosch-like paintings.

The Garden of Earthly Delights in the Museo del Prado in Madrid, c. 1495–1505, attributed to Bosch.

Allegoria na Amoreto – Stoimen Stoilov in the Foyer of the Varna University

Mostly the room features Iconography of the town and the castle of Gruyères by contemporary artists. The balcony off the room had a great view of the French garden and the pre-Alpine foothills.

Day two of the reunion weekend was to be lunch at a restaurant at Gruyeres famous for its raclette, known in the German-speaking part of Switzerland as Bratchäs, or "roasted cheese." Traditionally, Swiss cow herders used to take the cheese with them when they were moving cows to or from the pastures up in the mountains. In the evenings around the campfire, they would place the cheese next to the fire and, when it had reached the perfect softness, scrape it on top of bread. But it had to be served with wine or tea because water will make it harden in the stomach with big time indigestion.

I was never much on the dish when I was a poor student in Fribourg. It was hard enough to afford it then, but I figured lunch would cost somewhere around $50 and I had already packed a nice picnic from the exorbitant morning spread of breakfast at the hotel.

So, cheap skate Richard begged off the lunch part of the program thinking I would catch up with everyone at film showing at the castle at 3:30. I found a nice café that served cream-filled chocolate with the coffee and watched the passersby when it turned out I couldn't pick up the wifi in the town to continue my account.

Problem was that at 3:30 after I made my way with considerable difficulty back up to the castle, none of the group had arrived. Turns out lunch went longer than expected and they were still eating at the restaurant whose name I had neglected to take down. By about 5 I'd had enough people watching and decided to try to find the car in the parking. No luck. Battery dead on my cell. Nothing to do but put out the old thumb and see if I could hitch a ride back to Fribourg.

Fortunately, sweet Lynn and Mary Jo were standing at the entrance to the parking waiting for the others in their car to arrive. They put me in their car and called Charlie to tell him the lost had been found. So, feeling a little like idiot Jesus in the temple, I made it back to Fribourg and enjoyed the ride as Mary Jo rounded the roundabouts and drove her fancy rental car like a professional. At dinner, I somehow missed the meeting point as well, and spent the second night of the reunion on my own, re-visiting the café au Midi, thinking I might catch the group there.

I sat having Fondue for one, again, thinking they might turn up. I was treated royally by a handsome waiter and was just as glad to be on my own in a way. I had an extra room key which I gave him thinking he might visit after the restaurant closed. But he was only officially nice, and any day dream of scoring in Switzerland had to be put off till another day.

Once when William and I were touring Canada in my little orange Porsche, we called Louis Kronenberger who had a palatial summer cottage miles away from any town or official campsite and we were told we could drop in for a drink. When we got there, we were offered a martini at the cocktail party he was hosting for his houseguests and were sent on our way without even the offer of a shower of place to pitch our tent. We had been Kronnenbergered, a word that came to mean being given the shaft in a major way. "Once you have money, you can quite truthfully affirm that money isn't everything," he said famously in an essay, which gives you an idea of what a crank and snob he was.

By the end of the day at the castle, I felt a little like the guy in one of the paintings I saw earlier in the day in the Fantastic Art Room as I turned off the bedside light in my hotel room and thought of what tomorrow might bring.

But, sometimes a poem comes at night, sometimes early in the morning. And when you can not sleep, Nancy cures her insomnia by repeating poems that she knows as I did thinking of the time William and I were Kronnenbergered:

Canada Poem

It grew late, The Stars were
beginning to fall. We pulled off
The side of the road
And pitched our tent
In an open field.
Our sleeping bags
Were warm as toast.

In the morning
There was frost on the grass
And five beautiful cows
With large eyes
Wondering what had
Plopped down
In the middle of their pasture

15. SUNDAY BLOODY SUNDAY

If you look at process, I am at an interesting point right now. I'm looking at the past trying to have readers believe I am describing my feelings at that time. But they are filtered through the present. A journal is always that way I guess. Again, Wordsworth's emotions recollected in tranquility. But the effect of the elections on my spirit and where the country is going now really change how you feel about the past. If Trump had not won, I think my thinking about Switzerland would have been much freer and less depressed than I've been these past few days. Trying so hard to remember and recreate the Swiss weekend would have been easier. Interesting dynamic. Events in the present significantly influence what I think about the past and my feelings about it and how you present it. I'm sure psychologists have looked into how events influence one's emotional reality in the writing process, but I'm sure feeling it now.

Earlier in the book, I was willing to relegate Donald Trump and his big testicles to the dust bin of history. In a way, those two images still work. Now, he's bringing his big fucking testicles into the present and history. He's going to determine a lot. It's not that I am particularly afraid, but I guess I am concerned about what he will do for Gay rights, for women, for Hispanics, for blacks, you name it. But more importantly, one friend in the military feels he'll have us in a nuclear war within a month of the election. And I guess it is possible.

I think in one of my old wallets, I have some of those iodine pills they used to issue you in the event of an accident at our local nuclear power plant that are supposed to help counter the exposure to radioactivity. I ought to find them again, because, who knows … Imagine what it would mean, nuclear war. But even aside from Armageddon (in which case there wouldn't be much to worry about,) I think of what my future might look like at age 70. Am I going to spend my last good years fighting off the basket of deplorables that now control all branches of the legislative and possibly the judicial. Bye bye, Row v. Wade? Marriage equality in all 50 states? Gains in voter registration and protections. Imagine how my friend Peter Menike, Florida's Poet Laureate and his wife Jeanne feel being octogenarians and what the future means for their children and grandchildren. They'll be 90 and Trump could still be president. All the years of struggle and reform they worked for and committed themselves to would really be for naught in a way.

Time for a little medical marijuana as I ponder all this? But my chronology is already disrupted – no longer linear. The structure is turning into a spider's web. One thing that really has me pissed off in the present is the media. For months I followed MSNBC obsessively, every shift of the polls, the final reassurance that Clinton might even take the House and Senate. How could they have been so wrong? When you think of two consecutive Time Magazine covers showing Donald Trump's hair melting down – brilliant graphics, all wrong. Chris and Rachel and Joy should all be docked some from their salary for the grief they caused, how we hung on their every word, how we believed every poll they were reporting on, how it seemed to be in the bag for Hillary. FUCK.

The internet is a riot of self-congratulatory comments from the Trump people all calling now for peace and love and acceptance of Trump after the grotesque campaign he waged. Demonstrations all over the country don't seem to be letting up anytime soon and a million women may march the day after the inaugural. Peter Menke (Big secret is that he is to be the 2017 William Meredith Awardee for Poetry—there will be a press release by the time this book ever sees light of day, if ever) has written the following take on things in the Poets Corner he writes for in Creative Loafing out of St. Pete's in Florida. It includes a sketch by his wife Jeanne that will accompany the articles in his new book with us:

This election was an astounding victory for a party that did nothing for eight years besides attack Obama and Clinton, wasting taxpayers' money on phony targets, while setting back problems like climate change, education, and gun laws at least a generation. And now, encouraged by FBI Director James Comey's unprecedented double entry into this election with his late partisan bombshell — which may well have turned the election — the GOP has lowered the bar for allowable political behavior for decades to come. All we have left is *Saturday Night Live*.

ANYWAY, there I was at the New Hotel in Fribourg, waking up on a Sunday morning, the final day of the reunion weekend, hung over just the way I am in the present. Their wonderful buffet was some solace, and I was able to catch up with some of the gang to make plans for the day. Bob Nish was there, a guy I had hoped to spend time with anyhow, Bob had been to the cathedral for mass. He doesn't wear it on his sleeve, but as the Jesuits say, give us your children before they are two, and they are ours forever. I wondered how Bob's faith helped him deal with his wife's cancer and the extreme challenges he faced along with her when she was diagnoses with endometrial cancer. Four beautiful daughters, a slew of grandchildren, he didn't seem any worse for wear. What was going on in his sweet soul, I wondered.

"Bob, you guys visited the old dorm when you first came I understand. You want to take a walk with me today and show me where it is?"

"Give me fifteen minutes," he said and off we went in search of the Foyer St. Justin.

The guy at the desk showed us where to find the university on the map and so we began our hike up Rue de Pérolles. On the way, we talked about life and death. Some guys were playing bocce ball and Bob said he had begun to take it up recently at the suggestion of his yoga teacher, an Italian woman who apparently was becoming important in his emotional life. He gave me some of the details of how it had been for him and his wife – the enormous suffering, the many surgeries, loosing her leg, part of her pelvis, finally her life. How could he continue to be such a lovely, mild mannered guy. Incredible. For most of his career he worked with young offenders as a parole officer, magistrate, judge. A guy whose life was committed to good action based on his faith, but also fueled by his Irish spirit and background.

He turned out better than any of us as far as I could see. Middle class boy from Jersey, he starred on the basketball team, despite his short stature. Girls loved him for his smile and talent as a dancer. Just a sweet, modest fellow who made the world a better place for his life on the planet.

The further we got as we walked, the clearer it became that this was not the way to the university, that there were indeed now two universities in town and ours was in the exact opposite direction. With my bad hip and the extra weight I was carrying (which, come hell or high water will disappear this winter when I get to Florida and can ride my bike again) I was getting short of breath and suggested we take the bus back to the train station and start all over.

A friendly bus driver actually came out of the bus and showed us how to use the automated ticked dispenser then took our ticket and gave us instructions on which stop to get off at to find the university. He was more Japanese than Swiss for this desire to help someone lost in a foreign city.

Sure enough, in three stops after the train station, we found it. We could have been there in ten minutes had we not followed the concierge's instruction. But Bob was too much the gentleman to take issue with my map. No doubt about it. There were the two Saints on the façade of the building which now had become some sort of office building.

I remembered a circle in front that Doug Casey used to spin his Ferrari around throwing shale as he went for the pleasure of scaring the African students into the bushes. But it seems to have been replaced with a small chapel, Chapelet de la Divine Miséricorde which Bob and I dipped into. In the back of the church, there were cards with a picture of Jesus painted by the Polish nun, Soeur Faustine in 1931. Apparently, Jesus appeared to her in a vision and told her to paint an image of Him the way she saw Him, explaining that no one will ever be lost who venerates this image.

I said a prayer for Bob's wife, for Bob, for me for William. And we headed back to the hotel to make plans for dinner, taking in the town a bit as we walked.

103

As students, we sometimes met for Fondue Bourguignonne, a special treat in which cubes of beef (or sometimes horse meat we found out) are dipped in boiling oil and then dipped into a selection of sauces: curry sauce, garlic mayonnaise, pepper sauce, mustard sauce. If you forgot to transfer the meat from the fondue fork onto an eating fork, you only made that mistake once. The local pinot noir we drank with it was liquid gold, and the meal took on the importance of the last supper for us.

We decided there must be a restaurant on a rainy Sunday night that served this dish as it was to really be our last supper before moving on to wherever we were going on Monday morning. Charlie and Pat said they would join us but by the time we got settled in the restaurant, they were still an hour away from the day trip they took to Interlaken. We got settled and in no time Charlie and Pat came breezing in having pushed it to 100+ clicks an hour to get there.

Wiznewskki made an offhand reference to my needing a Baby sitter after yesterday's search party for me at the Chateau, but he always was somewhat of a cheeky little bastard, the class nerd, who seemed to make his fortune in some kind of secret government work. It was the kind of razzing an older brother might give, a verbal nuggie, and I let it slide. His zany animated theatre buff of a wife was a beautiful partner in what seemed to be decades of married bliss. Enough wine, and good food made for a family affair our last night together and at the end, I came into my own in a way. I was part of the pack, an alpha dog among a number of formidable alpha dogs, and at some level I still had the mystique of my Junior year abroad and didn't need to pretend I was anything but what I was.

16. SOFIA, HERE I COME READY OR NOT

The goal Monday morning was to get my butt to Sofia and this time I would not be spoon fed into the train and plane. I paid my bill the night before which I've learned is a good tactic so you don't get stuck in a line at the front desk of other people checking out at the same time.

I rolled my suitcase up to the train station and found the right platform. Once installed I took a snap of a nice-looking bald guy who I hoped would be on my train. But no such luck.

It was a rather improbable schedule I had set for myself, an itinerary that baffled Luftanza and required that the agents check several times to see if I had the right to do this. The game I was playing with them was to buy two separate tickets (one round trip from Dulles to Geneva) and a second one round trip from Geneva to Sofia. Since internal flights in Europe were less expensive than buying a single ticket that included the stops I needed to make. But what a hassle. The final day found me flying in and out of Frankfurt twice, leaving at 4 am and arriving in Dulles after a twilight Zone day of non stop flying in and out and back in again to Germany

Calendar for September Travel:

***Thur. 15 September 2016: DULLES/WASH DC–FRANKFURT

**Fri. 16 September 2016: FRANKFURT DE–GENEVA CH

**16–19 Met by Judy Cole and train to Fribourg

**19–20 Travel to Sofia

**Mon. 19 September 2016: GENEVA CH–MUNICH DE

**21 BLAGOEVGRAD : Travel to Blagoevgrad with visit to Rila Mona Staying at Phoenix Hotel

**22–28 Travel to Writers'Union House in Sozopol on the Black Sea. Travel to Varna during this week to visit Stoimen Stoilov and family.

**29 return to Sofia and staying at Rila Hotel

**Fri. 30 September 2016: GENEVA CH– FRANKFURT DE

**Fri. 30 September 2016: FRANKFURT DE–DULLES/WASH DC

The first leg of the trip went very well. I met a charming little dog named Lilly and had a good chat with a Tunisian girl who assured me the train I was on did indeed go to the airport. But she cautioned me not to get off the first stop in Geneva but to stay on the train until it dead ended at the airport. Janet Phoenix, a former student, gave me the rules for traveling: Keep moving, and ask a lot of questions.

The German airports I was connecting through were horrendous labyrinths miles long that were almost as bad as Hethrow and I vowed that I would take a wheel chair on the return to the US. I traveled with William this way in the old days, and we avoided missing any number of flights as a result. Once they book you for such special assistance, it is their job to get you to the plane on time. Given my shortness of breath at the long corridors and lugging the carry on with all the overweight books, it was a legitimate plan of action.

In Sofia, I was to be met by someone I had never met, Borislav Krustev, the son of the recently departed board of directors for the Meredith Foundation. Bobo's father, Valentin was one of the oldest friends William and I had from Bulgaria. He served as William's translator, in fact, the very first time William traveled to Bulgaria. We could always count on Valentin to translate any communication or collection of poetry. Guide, counselor, fellow poet, lawyer. He was a spectacular friend who translated not only the language but the culture of Bulgaria throughout our many visits to our second homeland. In fact, at the end of my Fulbright year in Blagoevgrad we were made actual citizens of Bulgaria, with red passport for external travel, and the internal passport as members of the EU. Here is President Zhelu Zhelev presenting after his decree and that of the Parliament making us citizens.

I couldn't imagine going to Bulgaria without Valentin to help us navigate the political and literary scene. But I wasn't sure his son was going to be willing to fill his shoes.

I was to arrive at late at night and I didn't want to have to confront the taxi cab sharks who would be patrolling the airport looking for a mark. And, sure enough, there he was, ready to accompany me to my hotel.

Once installed, we cracked some duty free, and I was able to pick his brain about what all had happened to our dear Valentin.

Perhaps he was still in shock, but I was curious about the objective way he described how his father had simply fallen over at his computer requiring their elderly mother to call the ambulance. Short and sweet—well I can't imagine a heart attack ever being sweet—but if you have to go, it is one step above slipping away in your sleep, or OD ing with hospice narcotics.

Bobo had followed in his father's footsteps as a translator and journalist and he was consumed with the country's elections. He said he tried to visit his mother routinely since she took it so hard. I am sure he took it hard too, but was putting on the existentialist face of an intellectual. He shared his father's penchant for attention deficit, but seems to have a kind of manic brilliance that was different than the studied, diplomatic personality of his father. He said they would at some point take his ashes to the sea and have a private memorial, like the trip I was making to the Rila Monastery with a small portion of William's ashes. I had hoped to visit his grave if there were on, but alas, no.

Several weeks before his death, we made Valentin our Bulgarian correspondent and board member of the Meredith Foundation. He was honored by the invitation and would have been such a great help. I wasn't sure Bobo had taken the time to see my tribute on our website, but before he left and I got ready to meet the Lion of Bulgaria the next morning, I pulled it up for him on the internet. I'm not sure what he made of the poem, but I was glad to have shared it with him.

IN MEMORIAM

It is with great sadness that we note the death of recently-appointed Board member, **Valentin Krustev** who died suddenly of a heart attack on June 3, 2016, at his home in Sofia, Bulgaria. This gentle spirit and brilliant intellect was friend, collaborator and cicerone to William and me for decades. He was an essential bridge between the foundation and Bulgaria and is irreplaceable. Here is my tribute to this dear friend and artist.

The Translator
      To Valentin

No word is too long until the word
comes that your are gone, and gone
now another world, another life
you brought me through translation.

Your art was like a window pane
Through which a reader met a poet
And his poem, with never a smudge
Of your own ego on the clear glass.

But it wasn't only the meaning,
it was the thing itself you showed me:
It was never a question of right or
Wrong: This simply is how we raise
our children, how we eat our soup.

A brash American overly sure of
Himself and his culture, learned a bit
The subtlety of silence, the elegance
Produced by history, the need and skill
to work and live in the hive at peace.

Quiet, master diplomat, smile on me again:
Translate me at the end of my own days.
The faults will be obvious enough.

I rely on your constant goodness, your talent
to intuit what I may have done well and speak
on my behalf brother, even if, at times, you must
"cloud the pane between us and the stars."

Valentin Krustev and William Meredith at Waterford Beach

17. LUNCH WITH THE LION OF BULGARIA

For two years, we had been hearing about the deteriorating health of our friend, the Lion of Bulgaria Lyubomir Levchev. He sent me an email saying he had been in the claws of several surgeries in Vienna but would be glad to welcome me on the 20th:

Dear Richard,
I just got your letter with great pleasure, and I would like to respond to you quickly, although not with all details. I asked my son, the talented poet Vladimir Levchev, to read me your letter and translate my response. I will be brief now, but soon I'll send you a longer letter. I will be happy to see you on the 20th at our place for lunch. My health condition does not allow me to meet you any place else. Anything that I can help you with, having in mind my health condition, I will do.
Looking forward to seeing you soon, yours,
Lyubomir

There had been so many rumors about this national poet of Bulgaria – Parkinsons, a stroke, unsuccessful hip operations – I wasn't sure what condition I would find him in and if this might be my final reunion with him and with wife Dora and their sweet "consigliore," Julia Malenova.

Lubomirs' friendship with William Meredith went back decades, from the times he was President of the Writers Union and invited William to several of the international writers conferences in Sofia. Valentin Krustev was the translator who first worked with William at the first Conference:

The meetings were sponsored by the Russians in fatter times and to some extent were simply propaganda vehicles from what I could tell. But the delegations did say what was on their mind in the era of Glasnost and Perestroika. Here is an entry from William journal dated September 25, 1980 which seems to be the rough draught of the type of official statements conferees were constantly being asked to formulate:

"I believe that the World Parliament of the Peoples for Peace will pass along to the International Conference of Writers at least one continuing challenge: namely, how hard it is to speak exactly, across the barriers of language and culture, of what is in our hearts. Everyone knows that the peace we talk about is more than its basic condition, the absence of war, just as truth is more than its basic condition, the absence of lies. This something more is what literature keeps alive in our imagination. Literature reminds us always of that great miracle, our common humanity. It gives us to do the beautiful and difficult work of keeping peace and telling the truth—tasks which only foolish people think will ever become easy."

In the Communist period under the dictator Zhivkov, Lyubomir was considered something of the poster boy for Communism and when Communism fell there was a moment when an angry public wanted to be off with all their heads.

Visiting good friend and poet Lyubomir Levchev, Bulgaria, 1984

(William Meredith meets Lyudmilla Zhivkova, Minister of Culture in the early 1980's)

One day in 1996, William and I sat looking out over the golden onion dome of the Russian Orthodox Church in Sofia waiting for our host, another famous Bul-garia poet to come into the living room. Georgi Djargarov entered, tall frail, cachectic and in pain with obvious cancer, but dignified and straight as a cyprus. He asked polite questions about my work, but the discussion quickly turned to his desire to get the record straight about his own role as the dictator Zhivkov's "vice president."

William Meredith, Georgi Djargarov and Richard at Writer's Union House in Varna 1994

I wondered if it were to be the same for Lyubomir. He has written a series of autobiographies warning when the guillotine went up, you would "be the next." And to his credit, Lyubomir refused to recant a lifetime dedicated to socialist ideals when called out by the Parliament. How could he, what would it have made him.

When we presented the 2013 William Meredith award for Poetry to Lyubomir, we did so to a poet, not a politician. The Russian critic Maxim Zamshev gives this rather subtle analysis in the prize-wining book GREEN-WNGED HORSE: "The poet has preserved throughout the years his understanding that the poet's force is in his ability to endure, to keep silent, to lead the readers along the serpentine paths of his poems, in the ability to turn temporary failure into a constant victory. Man has no right to lose: this is the figurative quintessence of Levchev's poetry of the seventies and eighties."

But when the Meredith Foundation awarded him the prize, it did so for poetry, a lifetime of verbal mastery and careful observation. "His speech is informed by a metaphorical vision of great beauty and power." I wrote in the introduction. "It is a unique voice, that of a poet, like his native Bulgaria, caught between past and future, East and West, who ultimately transcends these polarities. In those dark years after "the change," he was content to sing to the stars."

He asked me once when we visited Bulgaria to present the award, why the board had given it to him.

"It was given in honor of your friendship with William," I told him.

Ultimately, that personal friendship meant more than the all the past possibly murky business keeping one's head above water and out of the guillotine. Circles within circles. I've never understood what was actually going on in Bulgaria. Who could. Who can. Look how Trump is rising from the media ashes in our own country, how wrong the media was about his chances and what was really going on. Romney for Secretary of State after the vicious diatribes from both sides during the campaign. Who'd have thunk it.

William Meredith Foundation Treasurer presents Poetry Award to Lyubomir Levchev at the Sts. Cyril and Methodious Foundation

And so I was to fall into the trap of that same friendship that Lyubomir maintained between his family and William. I member how he fought me wildly when I tried to pull him into the surf one summer at the Black Sea, how hard he fought. Ultimately, I didn't manage it, and only found out later that he did not really swim. To think of this brilliant politician/poet now in his 80's and debilitated. Who could not fall into the trap of love. And now it was time for lunch.

I stood outside the balcony in the fancy building across from the Doctor's Park with paintings from friends such as Christo, Dora's friend from student days, and her own beautiful works including a winter scene and a recent portrait of Lyubomir. His eyes are searching, an indication perhaps of his present psychological state?

I found him in front of his walker, sitting in one of those special chairs that give you a boost if you need it to stand—which he did to embrace me. It was clear that he was "in there, knew me" as I wrote of a poem to William after his stroke. I had learned how to make small talk, or fill in the silences and this skill came in handy. I went on and on about my hopes for a memorial to William in Smoylan which Lyubo was trying to organize there with the Mayor. It seems the idea is still in the works from and email Lyubo sent me before my travel to Bulgaria:

"Several times I spoke with the mayor of Smolyan, Nikoloy Melemov. He sent a letter to the mayor of New London. In my last conversation with Melemov and others in regarding to the proposal for a monument to William in Smolyan it became clear that the idea is not abandoned. But because of constructions and other problems it may take place at the end of this year."

It was extremely moving to be with this dear old guy and national poet. It saddened me to think of his disability, but he was not to be counted out yet.

He asked me the how old William was when he died and I told him 88. Perhaps it meant a kind of competition and would give him the gusto to match William's longevity. He wasn't planning to go anywhere just yet as far as I could tell.

Some years ago I threw caution to the winds at a Greek festival where my favorite jeweler sold me a micro mosaic ring of Pegasus, symbol of poetry set in precious metals. After a fair amount of Rakia, I took it off and gave it to him, though I was cautioned by Dora that his hand was frozen into a claw and I needed to be careful when trying to put the ring on his finger. I managed it on his other hand. And he kissed the ring.

As usual, Dora had prepared a beautiful feast for us and we set to eating the delicious dishes.

At one point, a call came in and it seemed clear he was able to take the call and do business. The deep base voice and slow delivery was the same style I had witnessed so often when the big boss was taking care of business.

An earlier email confirmed that I would be welcome for a week at Sozopol on the Black Sea:

Dear Richard,

First of all, I would like to warmly greet you with your Birthday! For a poet —talented, brave and hearty, all praise is deserved. I believe you will forgive me for the one day delayed greeting.

I spoke with the leadership of the Union of Bulgarian Writers /especially with Hristo Ganov, Vice Chairman. It turned out that the second half of September the station in Varna does not work. However, new, more modern station Union in Sozopol will work and they will give consent for you to stay there – September 22–28.

And my email to the head of the Writer's Union confirmed my plan to come to the "rest house" after my travel to the Rila Monastery:

Dear Mr. Angelov,

My good friend and colleague, Krassin Himmirski has suggested I contact you about my plan to carry a small portion of William Meredith's ashes to the Rila Monastery in the afternoon of September 21. As you see from the following, I have written to the Abbot, but have not had a response so far. It may be presumptuous on my part to hope for a kind of benediction from the priests there, but I am driven to return to a spiritual center that was so comforting to me and William when we lived in Blagoevgrad. As I wrote Krassi just now,

I certainly plan to follow though on my plan to carry a small portion William's cremains on my own and offer them to the wind if nothing else. His spirit can ride the wind the way it blows through the heart of so many of his friends and lovers of poetry.

On the 22nd, Professor Vladimir Levchev has kindly offered to drive me to Sofia when I will take public transportation to Sozopol. I am very grateful to be offered a week's stay at the rest house of the Union of Bulgarian Writers. I remember well my last visit which was so kindly arranged by Nikolai Petev before his death. I hope to finish a short account of the past summer's activities titled REUNION while I am there. I will touch on the many dearly departed of the recent past and reflect on the growth of my own family as we look to the future.

I had originally envisioned this visit to Rila as a personal event, a kind of final farewell, but friends have suggested that it may have a larger interest among William's countrymen in Bulgaria. And I agree. Please feel free to contact me if you share this interest and I will be pleased to co-operate with you any way I can.

Meanwhile, I thank you for your consideration and send grateful very best wishes for the chance to extend my stay in Bulgaria.

>Sincerely,
>Richard Harteis, President
>WilliamMeredithFoundation.org

So, an exchange of gifts as usual, a call for a taxi, and promises to meet again after Rila.

18. SOZOPOL

So I have arrived in Sozopol and am sitting at the restaurant overlooking the Black Sea. Very beautiful and a little warmer this far south. It seems to be the last week of summer and things are beginning to shut down. A nostalgic time, but a time to think through this final reunion and put it into words.

Last fling at the beach before students return to the university

When I first arrived, I forced myself to walk to the "supermarket" up the road and buy provisions: Milk, cheese, bread, honey, olives, wine and gin, those great fava beans made with tomato sauce and fresh dill that are a delicious specialty here, Russian salad, Pepperoni, cashews, orange juice, a sponge, and laundry detergent. All for about $30. And I forced myself to do my laundry the way one does in Bulgaria: clothes on the shower floor as you shower and after in a small bucket to soak. Then hung on a clothes tree on the terrace to let the winds blowing off the Black Sea dry them through the night.

The apartment at the Writer's Union retreat

Vladimir Levchev picked me up a the little Phoenix Hotel after "Pancakes" which are actually crepes with jam and whipped cream. I had had my visit to the Rila Monastery and now it was time to continue on to Sozopol and the Writer's Union Rest House where I was to be billeted for a week, finishing up my tale of reunion.

We took only an hour to get to Sofia because of the new highway funded by the EU. Things are getting done because of the accountability when loans are made. Corruption, yes, 20% goes into someone's pocket, but at least Bulgaria has to show some progress for the money they are lent. The roads are remarkable between the major towns, but the back roads are a mess. They are hurrying apparently to meet deadlines before the snow falls.

But the road to the Rila Monastery when we drove up the mountain to place William's ashes was crowded with heavy moving equipment and men in blue overhauls directing traffic with little ping pong paddles, green and red to move the tourist buses in and out of the piles of stone and construction materials they were putting down.

In the car on the way to Sofia from Blagoevgrad, we talked politics, he explaining that Boiko Borisov, the current Prime Minister would probably put up a candidate at the last minute who would win. Boiko has been the leader for two terms now and has the best chance to win apparently. The five or so major parties have fractured into 10 or so, it seems. He is flirting with the Russians and keeping his ties to the west. Crossroads between east and west for centuries now.

Russia, of course, is just across the pond (Black Sea), but their pond is smaller than our Atlantic. Khrushchev apparently wanted even to sell Bulgaria to Russia in the old days, and it seems that a form of capitalism is already achieving that goal. One member of the Doma points out that Russia already has bought most of the Black Sea Coast and it seems to be true.

Even when we came here 20 years ago, Varna and the Golden Sands were a holiday resort for middle-class Russians, a place for teenage boys and girls to learn how to smoke and loose their virginity. The worry for Bulgaria, of course is that Putin will need to invade Bulgaria to protect Russian community taking root here, the way he claimed to do in the Crimea. But enough of politics. That may be down the road and as my father used to say when he was spending too much money, "50 years from now, it won't matter." Baba Vanga, the Bulgarian soothsayer says Donald Trump will destroy the US in 2017 and that Isis will invade us from Canada. In any case, the world will end in 2333 according to Vanga when meteors crash into the earth. So, we have a little time, at least.

In Sofia, we caught up with Lyubo, Levchev's driver who turned up in a red Mercedes van with his wife for the trip to Sozopol. I still can't figure if Levchev has paid for this travel on my behalf, or if, indeed, his driver agreed to carry me just out of friendliness.

Along the way, again fields and fields of sunflowers turning their black heads to the earth as fall approaches, the same fields that turned me nostalgic as I made my way to Sozopol in 2013.

The Sunflowers

The sunflowers bow their heads to the earth,
each the ghost of a summer joy, a lover's kiss,
the taste of rose and honey, a child's laughter.
The sunflowers are weeping at summer's end
seeds falling like black rain to nourish
and renew the spirit of the earth.

When lightning rages in the valley—
neon calligraphy on the black sky,
blue augury for winter and the freeze
to follow, they stand like Chinese
warriors awaiting rebirth or are
folded into the earth from which they
rose in the eternal cycle.

In spring, they rise refreshed, a
sea of yellow pleasure for new
lovers, replicating the DNA
of our love which gives birth to
children, and joy and sunflowers.

In the evening as I sat at the restaurant overlooking the sea drinking a glass of Rakia and eating the ubiquitous stuffed red peppers stuffed with cheese, I re-called Nicky's joke about the chef who ran out of cheese and took matters hand to provide the necessary stuffing for the peppers. But I won't go there…

From high above I watched a beautiful young man throw down his towel and begin to jog up and down the beach, ending with a swim and slow walk up the stairs to the modern part of the city. He was like a fine stallion, and I think of him now as the same sort of peeping Tom Hemingway must have been when he wrote his short story of Jake Barnes was it, who comes to a lake in Michigan and has a swim. I could have been that young man years ago, running effortlessly up and down the beach for my own pleasure, oblivious to the old men looking on in nostalgia and, yes, a kind of lust.

As I sit overlooking the last of summer in Sozopol, I think of the wonderful friends who helped me in my mission to the Rila Monastery. I think of beautiful Lydia who was such a wonderful friend to William and me the years we spent in Blagoevgrad. While I taught classes, Lydia spent afternoons with William and painted his portrait.

The day we went to the Monastery with William's ashes, she had dyed her hair eggplant color in William's honor the way Bulgarian women do and it looked really neat. She hobbled around the great stone floors of the monastery in her high heels which she wore strictly for the chic for William. Her long black dress and jacket made her look like a sexy nun from the monastery. But her face and eyes were puffy from chain smoking and water glasses full of vodka every place we stopped.

TRAVEL TO THE RILA MONASTERY

That morning, loyal Lucien agreed to drive us up to the Monastery. I was little miffed because the press people were coming to the Monastery at 2:30 and I wanted to leave enough time to have a nice trout lunch on our way up the mountain. Lucien was a half hour late. Turns out he was arranging for a sweet guy named Marti who has good English and is an artist to join us. Marti is something like Lydia's second son since her real son is I off working in Africa trying to get enough money to bring her black grand babies home.

Lucien Dimitrov at the American University in Bulgaria

Strange, lovely Marti was to be our translator then. Plucked eyebrows, diminutive figure, but with a wise, shy smile that makes one think of a seminarian. He might have been gay, but that was not at all clear. He is certainly warmly accepted and loved by the friends from Blagoevgrad.

The four of us began zooming up the mountain to the monastery, the car knocking us all about on the back road detour to the main road up the hill. When we finally arrival at the appointed restaurant for lunch, I placed William's ashes on the table and dressed the black velvet box with a small icon of Mary and the Christ Child and his Vaptsarov medal. So, he joined us for Rakia.

The press people came and began an interview but left us alone finally to have the beautiful trout. Rushing though lunch, I lost my stomachs in the rest room and sacrificed my underwear to the waste can. I remember Milton Bearle (uncle Milty, at age 80) looking into the camera on a TV commercial for Haines underwear, smoking a cigar and telling the camera, "At my age, I've done just about everything in my underwear."

Red peppers and white cheese. Yum

Since I had no word from the Archimadrate or whatever the proper title for the head abbot is, I was unsure what to expect. I lit a candle in front of St. Ivan's icon and wept, slight private heaving, and then joined Lucien in search of a priest. The cameras from national TV were denied permission to shoot within the actual church, and it seemed that everyone was out on some sort of retreat, but the woman (nun) at the kiosk selling icons made a call and suddenly a priest arrived. In the middle of the long explanations, I set William's ashes on a small table and the priest immediately knew what to do and took charge.

He was a beautiful man, about 45-50 with blond red hair, wearing a gold, sequined chasuble. I held onto an angel on a carved balustrade, as he sang alleluia and read in a cadenced ritual from a black book for about 30-45 minutes. He kept intoning William in the passages. And at the end, he packed up his book, I shook his hand and told him that now William rested in the arms of Christ. It was enough. He knew he had done his job: gave comfort to a grieving fellow pilgrim, and fulfilled a ritual he firmly believed in. There was no need to say anything else. We left the dark church and staggered into the sunshine.

The benediction went on longer than we had expected and Lucien had to return to Blagovgrad to teach his classes. But he left with promised to return for us. In the courtyard, we met the press, a sensitive reporter and a handsome camera boy – man, these Bulgarians are beautiful. I explained why we were here and he asked smart questions, particularly wanting to know more about William and this bridge he had established between our countries when he was the Poet Laureate of the US at the Library of Congress.

I had hoped to take the ashes to the cave-tunnel where by legend the Saint himself had crawled through and where now, if one made the same journey crawling through that dangerous space and made it through to the end, one's sins were forgiven. But it seemed too far away for the camera crew and so we walked a bit up the hill outside the monastery walls to find an appropriate place.

As we walked up the hill, a beautiful dog lay curled in sleep at the foot of the staffs that the monks had obviously prepared for hikers to borrow. The dog looked exactly like my own dog, Sydney, except that she was white where Syd-ney is silver. But the head and marking were the same. She was a mountain dog apparently, had come mysteriously from the hills and lived on the kind-ness of the taxi drivers and tourists who gave her scraps. I put out my hand and she seemed to know me immediately. She lifted herself from her bed and led us up the hill.

The camera man was joyful when he discovered the path leading up to a gravesite for the Irish patriot who did so much for Bulgarian culture at the turn of the century. It was a nice flat spot and the grave was quite impressive, but I turned my back to it: this was to be William's spot and I didn't want it to be associated with the Irish patriot.

I had kept William's ashes in a carved wooden box with a screw top lid that he had been given or pinched from an English cousin that time we visited her at the end of her life at Oxford. Later that night the camera man got a close up of the small white cloud as I poured his ashes into greenery along the pathway. We said the "Our Father" and returned to the monastery and a small café behind the monastery. More vodka for Lydia, more Rakia for me, and coke for Marti. I gave him now my coat because he was shivering and by then I was too. Lots of jokes about being abandoned, but it was getting serious. A taxi would take another hour to come for us. But the head of the parking, a man who had lived in Hyannis on Cape Cod, yet another beauty offered to take us back to town for $20 and in hopes his boss would not be back before then. He put us into a lovely warm VW and we were off, rolling down the mountain, dodging the massive trucks and blue-uniformed workers who would be there till 7 or later trying to meet the deadline of getting the road completed. The driver left me at my hotel so I got a good nap before we all met for a dinner at Diva, a popular restaurant along the river running through the Blagoevgrad. This was to be Lucien's treat and we told him we were going to have massive desserts when we caught up with him at Diva.

But before dinner and the nap, as the driver pulled up to the hotel, Marti rolled down his window and said to me, "We did something very good here today."

19. VARNA

Toward the end of my week in Sozopol, I was delighted to travel north to Varna, my favorite city in Bulgaria. My mission was to visit Stoimen Stoilov and his family, a family that had become something of my own Bulgarian family over many years.

William Meredith and I met Stoimen initially in Varna, on the Black Sea coast. He and his wife and daughter entertained us in the Atelier Vulcan, the studio he established which later grew to such fame for the biennial exhibition that was established at the museum. The reception we were given was very warm and the gifts of his art were generous. Both have continued now for decades.

Stoimen took his wife to Vienna for medical treatment and after she died, he stayed on in Austria where the government has recently awarded him the honorary title of Professor. At one point, he created a kind of "Where's Waldo" map of the metro system which was found at all the stops along the line in Vienna. At the end of red line, a man with wings carrying books on his back flew down to me and William. Stoimen put us there among Freud, Marx, Klimt, Frans Joseph and other denizens of the capital because it was the line to the airport where he went so often to meet our plane when we arrived to visit him.

Stoimen and his remarkable sister Margarita and daughter Diana, both fine artists in their own right, became Bulgarian family. Their generosity knows no bounds, and the gift of their art has graced the walls at Meredith Center as well as numerous book covers, illustrations, and broadsides.

In 2000, the Lyman Allyn Museum mounted a show of his work, and the heroic canvases were stretched in the museum itself. One of the works, Orpheus, taking its inspiration from Thracian legend was featured in the the Bridge of Light exhibition at the Slater Memorial Museum in 2015.

Orpheus, oil on canvas 2.5 x4 meters

Richard Harteis, William Meredith and Stoimen Stoilov Lyman Allyn Museum in the year 2000.

One important project we worked on together relied on the Disabled American Veterans and the Dominion nuclear power plant who commissioned a series of etchings "illustrating" the poem by Meredith memorializing the loss of 128 lives in the sinking of the nuclear submarine, SS Thresher in 1963. The poem and etching were sent to all surviving families of that disaster.

**Stoilov etching to illustrate the William Meredith Poem,
"The Wreck of the Thresher"**

On November 29, 2014 this project expanded into a permanent memorial for City Hall in New London for the brave sailors, many of whom came from our community. The following photo shows the New London High School Navy Junior Reserve Officer Training Corps Color Guard as it posts the colors during the Pledge of Allegiance at the start of the dedication ceremony:

Sea Guardian

Most recently, I got an announcement from Varna celebrating the heroic murals he had just completed: "The Academic management of the University of Economics- Varna has the great honor to invite you to the grand ceremony for the opening of the monumental paintings by the artist Stoimen Stoilov created in honor of the 95th anniversary of the University.

The event is on 29 April 2015, 16.00 at the central hall of the University of Economics – Varna. The paintings measure 4 X 4 Meters Website: www.stoimen-stoilov.com

I was very anxious to see these works and my old friend. I had a farewell dinner as the end of summer fireworks played over Sozopol, packed up my bags and found a taxi to Bourgas to catch a mini-bus to Varna. In no time, I was walking the streets of Varna with my old friend Stoimen who was my host yet again.

First order of business was lunch, of course, with Stoimen's sister Margarita, a fellow Leo who had celebrated her own birthday in August.

Then off to the University to check out Stoimen's latest masterpieces.

In a review of the Lyman Allyn Show, art critic Rick Koster describes how Stomen's works display a paradoxically futuristic interpretation of the mysticism and mythology appropriate to both eastern and western Europe.

"Fasten your seatbelt, and join the ghosts of other travelers who've apparently been inside his brain a while: Hieronymous Bosch, Albrecht Dürer, Pan and his eclectic and recurring entourage of Greco-Roman deities and myth-makers, Leonardo DaVinci and maybe the painter/patricide Richard Dadd."

Valeriy Poshtarov, writing in the catalog for the murals explains that "The major themes that concern him are related to the history of the Thracians and the ancient mythology, the cosmogony of the Bogomils. The pagan relationship of people with animals and the ritual offerings are displayed with sacred drama."

Margarita's husband Ivan (who looks a little like St. Ivan of Rila, as a matter of fact) is a psychiatrist. Unlike many of his countrymen who have become economic refugees in the west, he has stayed in Bulgaria to provide desperately needed help to his countrymen. It turns out Ivan is a Mason according to Margarita. In the costal town of Balchik, the Mason's were about to build a house when it was discovered that a General to Hydrian, his private physician, was buried there. Founded as a Thracian settlement, Balchik was later colonized by the Ionian ancient Greeks with the name Krounoi (renamed as Dionysopolis, after the discovery of a statue of Dionysus in the sea.)

To their credit, the government insisted that the archeological ruins be preserved in the building. The artifacts they found there are now in the archeological museum including instruments for trepanning. Amazing to think they were doing brain surgery thousands of years ago.

Since Margarita was being commissioned to paint the ceiling of the Mason's temple, Stoimen decided we should take a little excursion to Balchik to check out the scene.

But lunch first, of course, along the harbor.

And then, sadly, it was time to return to Sofia. Stoimen looked after my heavy bag despite his own recent hip replacement. What a tough, lovely guy. I took this shot of him waving to me as the bus was about to depart. "Bye bye, Richie." I could hear him say it in my mind's eye like so many times before over the many years of friendship and departures.

20. RETURN TO SOFIA

On the bus now with my little Ipad, trying to catch up. I wouldn't want to be driving this big bus. Ahead is a cement truck that he is trying to pass. I avert my eyes as William would say.

Tonight I hope to have dinner with Valentine's son. He never translated the piece I wrote about spreading the ashes at the real a monastery. But he did meet my plane which was a very big help and he has finally written to reassure me that I have not given offense in any way he is apparently just extremely busy covering the political landscape right now. So I was heartened by that email.

The hills now have that burnt orange quality from early fall. It looks like gypsy moths have begun shredding the trees. Here, as in England, the fall colors are very muted, a kind of dingy brown. I wonder why ours are so brilliant in America by comparison. The climate is roughly the same, and I don't think it has anything to do with the amount of water the hills get.

Now we have to pull over or stop for some reason I wonder if someone needs to pee very badly and seems to be the case I guess she didn't plan very well in terms of the amount of water to be drinking for a three-hour trip.

Anyhow, the colors make me think of William's Hazard The Painter poem in which Hazard goes sky diving to get the overhead perspective.

    Hazard's Optimism

    Harnessed and zipped on a bright
    October day, having lied to his wife,
    Hazard jumps, and the silk spanks
    open, and he is falling safe
    This is what for two years
    he has been painting, in a child's palette
    —not the plotted landscape that holds
    dim below him, but the human figure
    dangling safe, guyed to something silky,
    hanging here, full of half-remembered
    instruction but falling, and safe.
    They must have caught and spanked
    him like this when he first fell.
    He passes it along now, Hazard's
    vision. He is in charge of morale in a
    morbid time.
    He calls out to the sky, his voice
    the voice of an animal that makes not
    words but a happy incorrigible noise,

not of this time. The colors of
autumn are becoming audible through
the haze. It does not matter that the
greatmasters could see this without
flight, while dull Hazard must be
taken up again and dropped.

He sees it. Then he sees himself
as he would look from the canopy above
him, closing safely (if he can remember
what to do) on the Brueghel landscape.
Inside the bug-like goggles, his eyes water.

In front of me, a nice mother has profited from the travel time to do a little homeschooling. What an adorable little boy she has. The family is on its way to visit Rupite, where the soothsayer Vanga lived and told the future. The father is from Varna and they have been fed the official line about her and the hero poet, Vaptsarov, and the nostalgia for ancient Bulgaria.

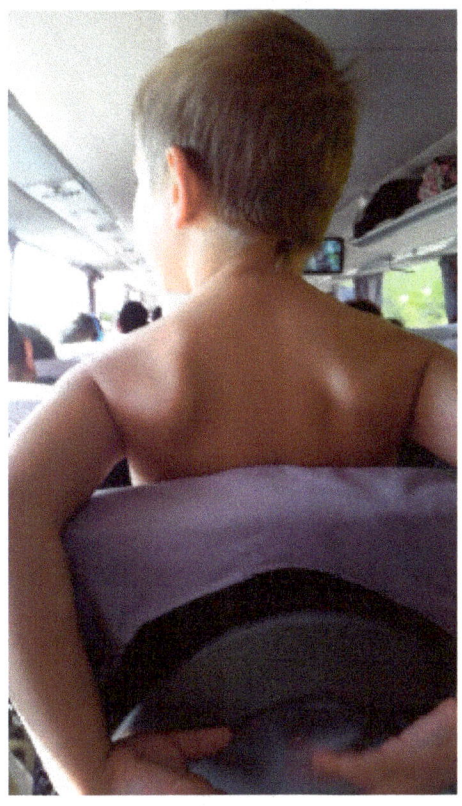

I guess I'll always regret not having had children. When I see this little boy, I think of the terrible tragedy at Sandy Hook. This little boy must have been about the same age as those children. I was on Fishers Island teaching the day when it occurred, and I recall the child in the computer room who said to me at the end of the day, "Look what happened!"

Sandy Hook Revisited

For Anne Mari Murphy
Christopher Dylan Hockley
And Senator Chris Murphy

As he was learning to read
To read people, and to read life,
To know what danger is, to
Know what is needed to succeed:
All the big lessons, in came
A monster, who began slaying
The playmates the boy was
Beginning, at last, to play with.

This was not a storybook monster: Real
Slaughter everywhere—how could you
Trust anything, if you already had
Trouble trusting what it meant to be a
Friend, to trust his eyes.

          She took him
In her arms, to give him a flickering
Moment of fragile reassurance, being
Human, loving each other, how we
Need to play today, she lied to him—

In his confusion, she was able to give him
This moment of hopeful distraction
Before the bullets cut through them both
Like a sword. And she wrapped him up with a
Mother's instinct, and they left us like angels to
The sky, to the unknown.

A makeshift memorial on Berkshire Road in Sandy Hook

21. MEET THE PRESS

The final day of my reunion summer in Sofia, I had one more invitation to take care of before the flight home. Lyubomir suggested one more visit, a drink in the afternoon to meet Angela Dimcheva. During my week in Sozopol, there had been a lot of press coverage beyond the National TV account.

https://www.youtube.com/watch?v=Ryy2K3WTs9Y

The major newspaper, LABOR, had assigned Angela to cover Lyubomir's recuperation and monitor the people the great man was meeting with.

Once in Morocco, when William and I met Paul Bowles living in the Medina, he explained with a zany, Terry—Southern cheekiness that the world came to him now, and that he hadn't been out of bed in two years. In the literary world in Bulgaria, there was no one who had achieved Lyubomir's public stature. His story, was the story of the country in a way.

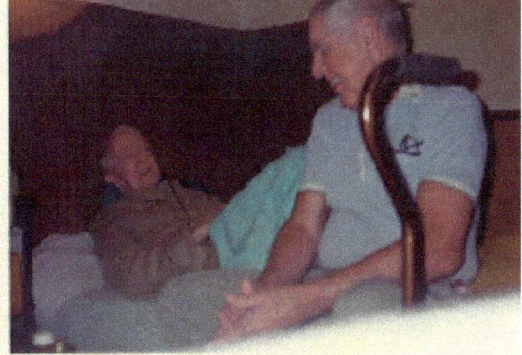

Visiting Paul Bowles in Tangier, April 1993

She was a lovely woman, cordial and geneous with the material she was presenting.

Loyal Julia presented me with all the newspapers that had been reporting on the Rila Monastery trip and our various meetings with Lyubomir over the years. Angela's Dimcheva's feature article drew heavily on the history of our visits to Bulgaria and friendship with Lyubomr. She later received an award for this coverage.

The other major papers covered this visit as well, but I was glad to have photos from the most recent time in Rila:

Мередит

▲ Ричард Хартайс, Дора Бонева и Любомир Левчев след връчването на Международната награда "Уилям Мередит" на нашия поет – 25 май 2013 г., София, в сградата на Международната фондация "Св. св. Кирил и Методий".

▲ Ричард Хартайс представя сборника със стихове от Л. Левчев, преведени на английски: "Green-winged Horse" ("Кон със зелени крила").

▲ Мередит, Хартайс и Левчев в София през 2005 г.

негови близки приятели. През 1981 г. представлява САЩ на тържествата за 1300-годишнината на българската държава. Участва в няколко от Софийските международни писателски срещи.

През 1983 г. Мередит получава тежък инсулт, който го парализира да превежда, да работи за каузата на американската и българската култура. Точно тогава издава антологията на българската поезия "Прозорец към Черно море", през 1986 г. излиза редактираният от него сборник "Поети от България", съдържащ 73 стихотворения от 24 съвременни български поети, преведени от Джон Ъпдайк (носител на над 20 престижни награди), Ричард Уилбър (носител на "Пулицър"), Максайн Кюмин (поетеса лауреат на Конгресната библиотека) и самият Уилям Мередит. Той е носител и на Наградата за литература на в. "Лос Анджелис Таймс" за книгата си "Частична равносметка: Нови и избрани стихове". През 1997 г. печели Националната книжна награда за поезия за "Говор с усилие".

В началото на 90-те години, когато у нас започна клеветническата кампания срещу Вапцаров, не друг, а Мередит застава с царствен жест зад името на нашия поет, като поръчва да му позлатят медальона с лика на Вапцаров и гордо го носи непрестанно до смъртта си на 30 май 2007 г.

В продължение на 36 години до поета неизменно е неговият приятел Ричард Хартайс. Заедно прекарват месеци в България, работят в Американския университет в Благоевград, а посещенията в Рилска обител са така необходимото откровение за ранимата душа на всеки творец. Двамата стават български граждани през 1996 г. "Ако случайно умра в тази прекрасна страна, нека ме погребат в манастира", казвал Мередит. И ето че 9 години по-късно Хартайс изпълнява тази негова воля.

Още през 2007 г. Ричард Хартайс оглавява Международната фондация "Уилям Мередит", която спонсорира книги, изложби и други културни проекти в САЩ и по света. И сътрудничеството с България продължава. На 25 май 2013 г. в София поетът Любомир Левчев е удостоен с Международната награда "Уилям Мередит". Тя представя сборник с избрани стихотворения с интригуващото заглавие "Green-winged Horse" ("Кон със зелени крила").

Кое предизвиква този интерес към нашата култура? Както пише в официалната грамота, това не е само признание на таланта на Любомир Левчев, но и на неговия живот, посветен на културните процеси в България и САЩ: "Тази награда отбелязва неговото словесно майсторство, остра наблюдателност, мъдра проницателност и мъжество; в неговите метафорични стихове звучи един уникален глас между миналото и бъдещето, между Изтока и Запада, който преодолява крайностите. Наградата е признание не само за таланта на Левчев като поет, но и за братството в областта на изкуството, за вярното приятелство, което Мередит и Левчев изпитваха един към друг през десетилетията. Между двамата поети може да има само светлина..."

Какво са наградите за един поет? Статистика, която публиката едва ли ще запомни. Но няколко поколения американци знаят наизуст стихотворението на Уилям Мередит "Голямата творба". Повтарят го и българските почитатели на поезията, които често отгръщат билингвистичната стихосбирка "Сияйните наблюдатели", издадена от ИК "Орфей" през 2003 г., или томчето с негови стихове "Пристрастни описания" (ИК "Орфей", 2008), в което като виртуозни познавачи на американския стих и на поетическата интерпретация са се включили Валентин Кръстев, Владимир Филипов, Корнелия и Божидар Божилови, Иван Голев, Валери Костадинов, Владимир Левчев, Георги Белев, Богдан Атанасов и Кристин Димитрова.

I had dinner by myself in the hotel that last night since Valentin's son was too taken up with the elections. I had an impossible day of travel ahead of me, starting with a wake up call at 4:30. The restaurant had been taken over by a party for a very large lady having her 60th birthday. I sat listening to all the pop songs from the 80's and 90's and some folk music as well. Before I went up to pack, I met her and gave her a little icon that I had attached to the velvet box of William's ashes. As I packed my bags, a knock came at the door. It was my waitress who was carrying a piece of birthday cake. "You didn't have any dessert," she said.

I was proud of what I had accomplished for my two friends, but now it was time to wing my way home.

22. EPILOG: Super Moon

William has a wonderful poem in *Hazard The Painter* titled, "Winter, He Shapes Up" in which he writes

> Today the first snow fell.
> It hung in the hollow air
> making space tangible,
> showing him how things are.

So it was for me when I woke this morning and looked out at the first snow dusting the lawn.

The last lines of the poem tell the tale as I struggle to finish this account and move into the future.

> Though more of each day is dark,
> though he's awkward at the job,
> he squeezes paint from a tube,
> Hazard is back at work.

I returned to America and a Supermoon, the closest Supermoon since 1948, just about the time as I was born 70 years ago. This fall, I stood out under the moon like a goblin and took a photo of the moon glowing between the limbs of a tree, yoked in the yoke like our friendship William wrote about in his poem, "A Couple of Trees."

> *How perilous in one*
> *another's V our lives are,*
> *yoked in this yoke: two men,*
> *leaning apart for light, but*
> *in a wind who give each*
> *other lee*

The internet gave a cheeky little solution to seeing it if you happened not to live in the country and were stuck in the ghetto somewhere.

Just in case you can't see the super moon.
A large tortilla on the window does the job

One of my favorite commercials when I got home to American TV was for an insurance company selling homeowners insurance. The guy goes in and tries to file a claim for his air conditioner. The agent wrinkles her nose and says no, "air conditioners aren't covered in your home owners." "Well what is covered," he asks." Well, things like an earthquake, floods, a zombie apocalypse…." In the window outside her office we see zombies stumbling around and a woman who is not a zombie screaming, "Zombie Apocylapse!"

My sister Barbie likes to follow the conspiracy theories that come out of Pa Dutch country along with hexes, pot pie, blood sausage, etc. Things like the United nations taking over the country, black helicopters. She went to Medjorie, for example, to see the nightly visit by the BVM and the glowing of the cross as you climbed up the mountain in the middle of the Bosnian War. Her husband refused to send her, so she got a group of women together and they paid for her travel. She's big into Padre Pio and the smell of roses accompanying sainthood. Anyhow, one urban legend I've heard though her is that the end of days will come when there is war in the mid-east, and a TV celebrity becomes president. Maybe she is onto something. Hello.

Seems we've had a zombie apocylapse. A whole nation of deplorables, not just a basket of deplorables, and Trump is now scheduled to be our president. Two people I admire very much wring their hands over the question as well as thousands demonstrating across the nation. Peter Meinke writes in his Poets Notebook:

This election was an astounding victory for a party that did nothing for eight years besides attack Obama and Clinton, wasting taxpayers' money on phony targets, while setting back problems like climate change, education, and gun laws at least a generation. And now, encouraged by FBI Director James Comey's unprecedented double entry into this election with his late partisan bombshell — which may well have turned the election — the GOP has lowered the bar for allowable political behavior for decades to come. All we have left is *Saturday Night Live*.

And Chris Murphy, our hunky smart Senator from Connecticut, writes:

Last night hurt. Never in our lifetime has a candidate for president run a more hate-filled, bigoted campaign. It felt like we took a step backward in our progress toward a more compassionate, inclusive nation. But that doesn't have to be our fate. We can choose to take Donald Trump at his word last night and take steps to heal the wounds caused by this bitter and divisive election. We can refuse to reflexively back ourselves into a dark, angry corner, and choose instead to be fair-minded umpires—calling the balls and strikes as we see them, working with our new President when he proposes good, and fighting him like hell when he proposes bad.

Another bit of wisdom from the internet suggests:

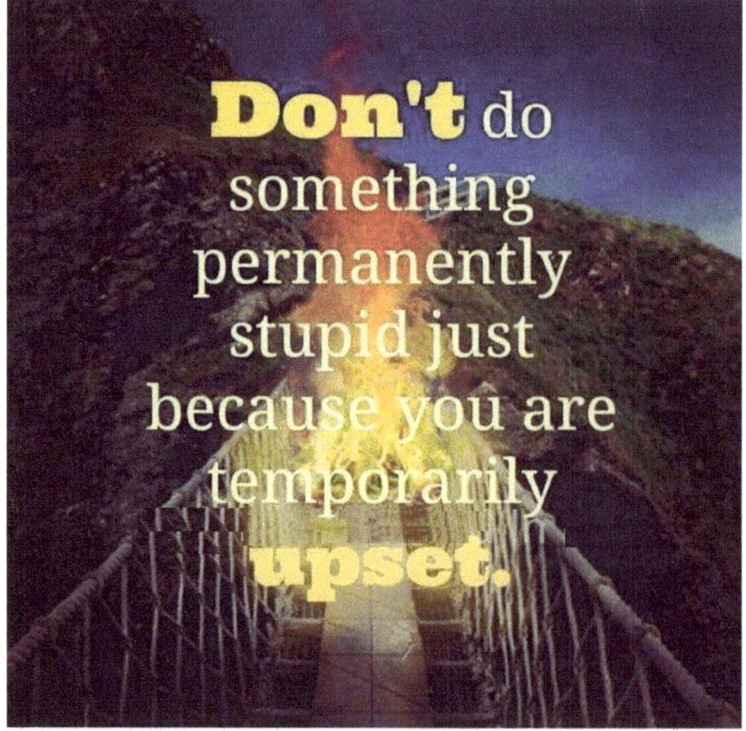

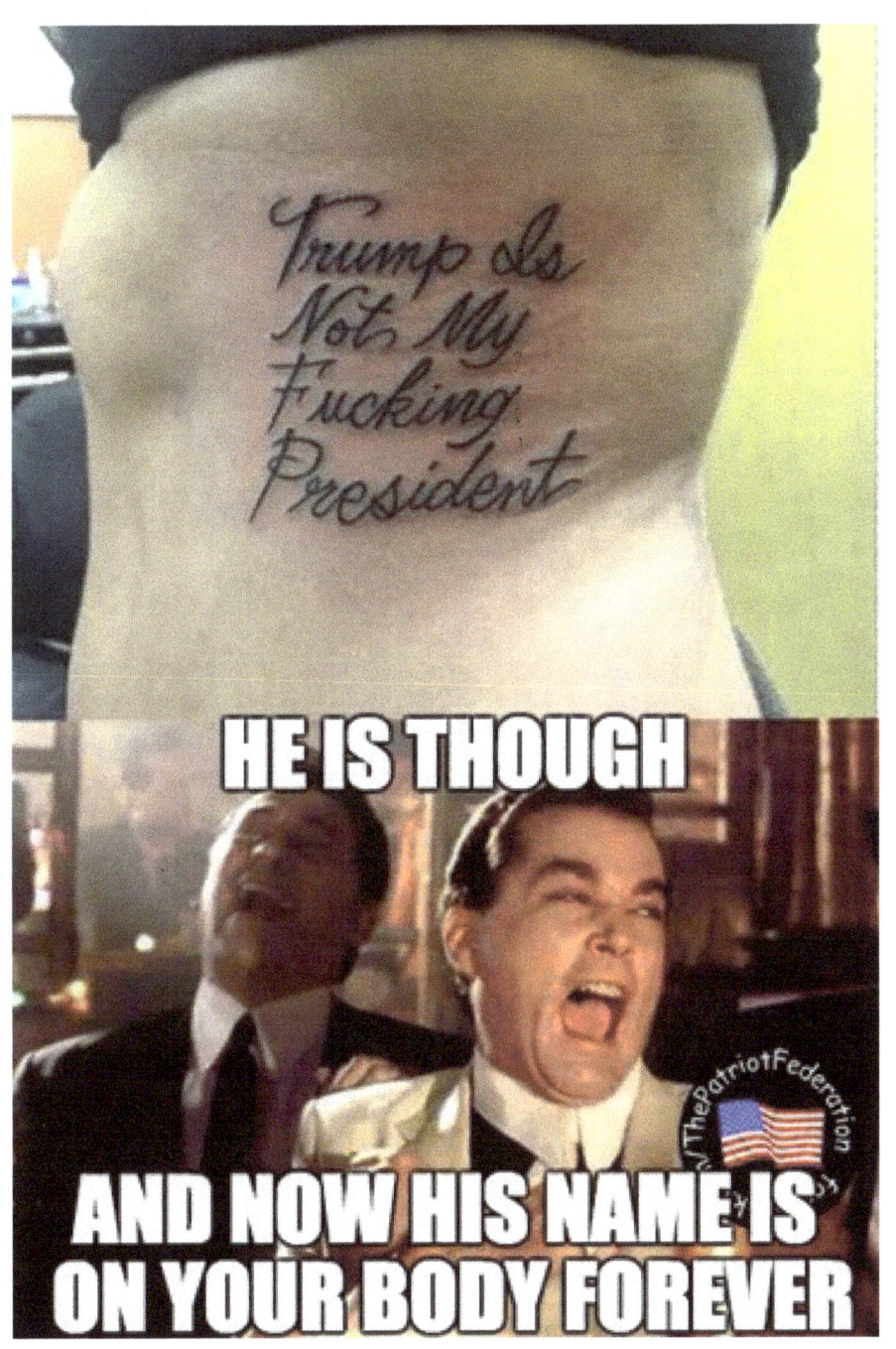

The day after inauguration, DC is looking for a million women march to protest his misogyny among other deplorable positions.

Artist, Casey Spectacular dresses as Zombie future at Halloween

Hillary Clinton stood for all the right values, she probably still has her health, she's got plenty of money, and she certainly retains her stature in the culture. You can't blame her if her initial reaction was to throw some plates around and scream a bit. There will be a woman president someday. It doesn't have to be her and there is no necessary urgency about it. It really does come down to the qualifications of the person. Everyone was hyped this time around, especially women, and I can understand that. But the necessity isn't there yet.

My thinking is, "well, he won, though not fairly as I see it. What can we do but just give him a shot and see what he does, though I can't help but feel he is just mooning us big time, to follow the super moon theme here.

Let's see what happens. Maybe it will all be smoke and mirrors like the "Fast Eddie" who pays premium money for your gold. Eddie has ropes pulling up his cape to make him seem like he is flying, like the Wizard of Oz.

A beautiful poet named Martin Galvin that we are now publishing has a line from his poem "Fourth of July at the VFW" which seems prescient:

> The crowd stirs its last eyes
> into the dark and hearing only fffft
> Turn to their empty cars, their sights
> Fixed on a better time than this.
> Above them, the moon bucks and rears
> in its traces, throwing the ocean around.
> Stars that went out before we began
> steer them on their way

Sydney and I will have to go to Florida and try to remain incognito since we live just across the intra costal from Trump's winter palace, Mar Y Largo among a lot of deplorables on the Board of Directors at my condo.

We'll keep a low profile like the cool dude on TV who drives a Volvo and like the crafty fox owns the east and west, north and south, and all will be beautiful to me.

Sydney and I will come back in the spring and she can guard the point from the swans again this summer.

And the next Supermoon will come January 2, 2018, just in time for the mid-term elections. Perhaps by then things will have worked out.....

www.ingramcontent.com/pod-product-compliance
Lightning Source LLC
Chambersburg PA
CBHW061928290426
44113CB00024B/2844